KANBAN

A Beginner's Project Management Guide:
Learn Kanban Method In Simple And Easy
Steps Starting From The Basics

Mike Smith

Table Of Contents

INTRODUCTION

Productivity is the one thing all of us want to improve, especially when it comes to work. It's what will get us through our tasks and objectives so that we can complete the overall goal and finally be done with it.

But projects can be challenging to tackle, especially when you find that they're not the kind that have you go from point A to point B easily. In fact, when you decide to take on a project, you'll see that point A goes to a different point than B, and then another, and then another. Soon, you'll find yourself zigzagging between more points than you planned to.

Don't worry, there's a way to get yourself out of the rut and manage your projects easily: Kanban.

Kanban: A Beginner's Project Management Guide: Learn Kanban Method In Simple And Easy Steps Starting From The Basics is the eBook that will show how the Kanban method works and how you can apply it to your various projects. Whether it's for personal or professional reasons, you'll find the Kanban method will get you to the results you've been wanting for so long.

So, what should you expect to read in this eBook? Here's a brief overview of what you'll be seeing as you go along:

Chapter 1: What Is Kanban? tackles the overall meaning of Kanban and its brief history. You'll learn a bit about how Kanban was formed and its evolution to the current form that you'll be learning about in the later chapters.

Chapter 2: Why Use The Kanban System gives you an idea of why you should use Kanban in the first place. This chapter will also let you know the various benefits and risks that you'll need to learn by heart.

Chapter 3: The Kanban Methodology digs further into the ways Kanban is applied in various areas, as well the different system types, mistakes you'll need to avoid, and importance of the Kanban board.

Chapter 4: The Kanban Board is where you'll find out more about the importance and value of the Kanban board. From the way to set it up to some of the things you need to do and not do, you'll see why you'll be using this more and more as your project moves along.

Chapter 5: Kanban's Application is where you'll learn where Kanban is applied. You won't only learn the usual areas it's used, but you'll also see how it has been applied in the unlikely areas you would have never thought of. You'll even see a few success stories that prove Kanban provides a way to achieve success for teams that look like they have no hope left.

Chapter 6: ABC Classification discusses a concept in Kanban that may be a bit confusing and daunting to understand at first, but with the explanation on how it works and the process that brings it all together you'll see why it's essential.

Chapter 7: Kanban Versus Other Systems is where you'll compare Kanban and other systems that help you manage projects. You'll see the differences, how they compare when it comes to efficiency, effectiveness, and more.

Chapter 8: Scaling is where you'll learn what you'll need to do to make scaling work when using Kanban. Many will claim that scaling can't work in Kanban, but with a little ingenuity, there's a way.

Chapter 9: Certification is the chapter to go to when you want to finally go for it and become a certified Kanban expert. Here you'll learn about the official certifications that are recognized worldwide. You will also learn a few good tips about boosting your skills.

Chapter 10: Doing Kanban Solo is where you will learn how to practice the Kanban methodology on your own. It may seem like a crazy concept to begin with, but with a little tweaking here and there, you'll find Kanban can indeed be adapted on your own.

Also, if you're eager to learn ways to make sure you're up and running with Kanban, the chapter **Notes** has it all for you. You'll learn where to get the certifications you've learned about in Chapter 7 and know the programs that will be a great help when using Kanban.

If you're ready to learn how project management works using Kanban, then read on!

CHAPTER 1:
WHAT IS KANBAN?

When you read or hear the word "Kanban," does it make you think of anything? Does it seem familiar to you? If your answer is no, it's okay. For the majority of people out there, Kanban isn't exactly a familiar word. But what you may not be aware of is that Kanban has been used in project management for decades.

So, what is Kanban? It is a Japanese word that roughly translates to "card you can see" in English and is mostly known now as a visual card system. Kanban helps you visually map out your workflow and processes for your project. Another way to put it is it's a scheduling system that leans toward visualization. It may have an odd name, but the project management system it provides makes up for it tenfold.

History of Kanban

Kanban started out back in 1940. Developed by Taiichi Ohno, an engineer and businessman for Toyota in Japan, Kanban was created to be a system for planning a project's goal, managing aspects of inventory, and working effectively and efficiently.

But how did that come to be? At the time, Toyota's performance with regard to productivity wasn't something to write home about, and their American rivals were at the top of the automobile production industry game. So, Ohno was assigned to create a system that could put Toyota's production line back in full swing.

It was said that Ohno came up with the concept of Kanban when he took note of an idea after going to the supermarket. As he realized, one establishes a time to go to the supermarket when they're in need of supplies, like food, liquids, and other essential items to keep themselves going for the week. Going to the supermarket occurs because the stock has run out. So, naturally, the person will resupply. On the other side of this cycle, the supermarket will now notice the shelves that contained the products they're selling might be running out, so they'll resupply them. In a way, it's almost like looking at the classic case of supply and demand.

It then occurred to Ohno that visual signals were present in the case of supply and demand. This became significant because it was the way to prompt people to go through the process and it showed him the power of pull systems. In a way, Ohno began to see that what supermarkets did was what happened with many production processes.

Ohno then identified the flaws of Toyota's production line and began to seek solutions for better ways to make production more efficient. Seeing as how the company he was working for dealt with cars, he thought that trying to move so many parts with the tools and methods they had at that time was inefficient, which meant productivity levels were very low.

So, with the supermarket idea put to the test, Ohno and Toyota adapted what they could with the notion so that they could help the workers become more productive at their tasks.

This method also allowed Toyota e to let the workers know who was in charge of certain aspects of the production process, what was needed at the time, and where the limits were.

In time, Ohno also began to make use of the visual signals he associated with supply and demand through the use of cards. This was where the early concepts of "To-dos" and other ideas that would define and build today's form of Kanban would come from. These visual signals were a way for the production floor to communicate so that when workers needed something to do, they already knew what the current progress was.

Because of Ohno's introduction of Kanban, Toyota was able to bounce back and achieve their goals with respect to productivity. It gave them a system where they could be efficient and flexible with the things they were producing while keeping the costs low and making sure to finish everything on time.

From then on, the Kanban system began to spread, and in no time other companies began to take note of Toyota's method. Today, there are hundreds of companies who still follow the simple concept of Kanban.

How Does It Work?

Kanban works with five core principles that have kept it going for decades. These principles are:

1. Visualize the workflow

When implementing the Kanban method, it's important to note how it will be adapted to the specific project. That's why the first principle is to visualize the workflow, which means you will map out what your project's steps will look like. It's a matter of imagining how the project will go before you start.

To do this, you create a Kanban board. Simply put, the board is a tool that can help you and your team visualize the workflow. You can't just keep it as a mental image, you have to make it a reality. So, the board is a way to take your ideas for the project and draw them out for everyone else to see.

Here's how a visualized workflow on a Kanban board would look like:

You'll learn more about the Kanban board in Chapter 3.

2. Implementing work-in-progress (WIP) limits

The next principle to follow is implementing WIP limits. This is important to take note of because it's easy to get overwhelmed with the growing number of tasks and goals that you'll need to achieve to get a project done.

By having the WIP limits set, you'll be able to set the pace and control how the tasks will be done. It'll also help you understand what aspects of the project must be adjusted to get everything done in time.

3. Being explicit with process policies

The third principle to follow is being explicit with process policies. It might seem extreme when you first read about it, but it'll be easy to grasp because when it comes to Kanban, it pays to remind yourself and the rest of your team the ways you'll process everything in the project you're managing. This is because it'll help everyone understand the expectations, the tasks, the WIP limits, and other important factors that will ensure the success you all aim for.

4. Measuring and managing workflow

The fourth principle to follow is making sure you're monitoring the workflow closely. With the workflow visualized, it's good to have metrics and other measuring tools that will show you how effective and efficient your methods are. It will also allow you to understand more about how tasks measure up with other tasks with regard to pace. This will help you determine if certain parts of the workflow are lagging behind while others are advancing at a steady pace.

5. Recognize improvement opportunities with models

The fifth and final principle to follow is recognizing the opportunities you see for improvement with models. This is where you'll analyze areas through various visual models that can show you where you and your team can improve. Whether it's through a chart or a spreadsheet, it'll help you see what parts of the system you can keep or remove to improve workflow.

These five principles may seem irrelevant to your current or future project, but when you integrate them to fit the unique specifications of the project, you'll see how handy they'll be when you finally start implementing the Kanban system.

CHAPTER 2:
WHY USE THE KANBAN METHOD

Now that you've learned what the Kanban method is all about, the next question you'll ask yourself is: Why use it? Managing a future project might seem simple to you right now, but when you finally dive into it, you'll find it's actually a difficult task. You may find your assumptions will be crushed when you find out what the project you're about to tackle actually requires to succeed. That's why you use the Kanban system.

Advantages

Kanban has many advantages that will help when it comes to project management. Here are some of those advantages:

- **You'll get flexibility**

  An advantage many are thrilled to gain when using Kanban is flexibility. A lot of projects can be too rigid to deal with because you're not sure if the tasks you're assigned can work when different circumstances come about or if the time frame is possible within the current scenario. But with Kanban, you'll be able to make adjustments on the go and still get things done.

  This is especially true when the situation calls for swift changes and tiny adjustments. After all, you can't expect a customer to have the same attitude toward a certain product that you and your team do. You also can't assume that your inventory will never fluctuate.

That's why with Kanban, you'll be ready to make adjustments when the situation calls for it. Need to adjust the time needed for a certain task to get done? Go for it. Have a workflow that might not work for the upcoming inventory resupply? Done.

The flexibility you gain with Kanban will help you respond to the ever-changing atmosphere of your projects. So, even if one little factor shakes things up, you can still get things done without losing the overall objective.

- **You'll have improved visibility**

When it comes to the Kanban method, visualization is vital. That's why one advantage you'll gain is improved visibility. While average project management systems let you have minor visuals, such as sticky notes, Kanban goes beyond that and makes the visuals essential.

So, your visibility on the overall structure of the project, along with the backlogs, the processes, and other data, will no doubt show you that you now have a better picture on where the project is finally heading to.

- **You'll be able to improve workflow efficiency**

Another great advantage of using Kanban is improving workflow efficiency. When you've visualized your workflow and gained better visibility, you'll get more things done. This means that the hassles, bumps, and other hiccups you had to experience with your project can all be scraped to the side because you'll have a better idea on what needs to be done to get your project completed on time. In short, you can get done with what you set out to do and be finished without breaking a sweat.

This will also help you honor the fifth principle of Kanban you learned in Chapter 1, recognizing improvement opportunities with models, because you'll be able to identify some of the areas in the project workflow that need to be addressed. And when you do that, you will significantly improve the efficiency of the workflow.

- **You'll be able to achieve ongoing delivery**

A great advantage you'll get with Kanban is being able to maintain ongoing delivery. This means being able to get all the things you've assigned in a project done in small portions to achieve steady output. It will also gain magnificent trust from your customers, clients, or superiors because it will show that what they expect from you will be done without any worry of delay.

- **You'll have better focus**

Focus is always important to have when you're doing important tasks, but sometimes it's hard to really concentrate on that when doing projects these days. You already have the tasks in mind, but when you're in the middle of it all, you'll find yourself and the rest of your team switching back and forth between tasks and not get anything done at all. That's why using Kanban will give you the benefit of having better focus.

How you ask? With your process policies and WIP limits implemented, you and the rest of your team will be able to set forth what is most important and get those tasks finished before moving onto the other tasks. This will also help you develop your focus on doing singular processes, so when all is said and done you can see that you've finally finished what you set out to do.

- **You'll achieve increased productivity**

Another great advantage you'll get with using Kanban is increased productivity. This means you'll finish the work you've started because why go through a project that just keeps going on and on without an end to it? The Kanban system will show you that you can gain the closure to the project you manage by being able to set the measure to which you'll start until you finish.

You'll also be able to learn the ways of measuring how long it will take to get tasks done and how to measure how many tasks can be done within a certain time. This data will help you understand how fast and effective everything needs to be to get your project finished on time.

- **Wasted work and time will be reduced**

With Kanban, you gain the advantage of reducing wasted work and time. This is quite beneficial because it means the worries of overproducing, waiting, over processing, and other forms of wastes in production terms will all be scrapped from the workflow. Instead, you'll be left with what is essential and be able to improve on what has been given to you.

This advantage has been a long-running tradition for Kanban because it was the main element that helped Toyota improve their manufacturing process. Creator Ohno himself identified different types of wastes in the processing line that he advised to be taken out as he was developing Kanban in the 1940s.

- **Predictability chances are raised**

When you're managing projects, it pays to know whether or not the chances of succeeding are high enough. Will you be able to make the delivery on time? Is the inventory ready for another re-supply? The advantage of using Kanban is that the chances of predicting correctly are raised quite considerably. What this means is there's certainty to be had in the process, which is rare when compared to most project management methods.

This also gives you the opportunity to make use of historical data, where you can see what worked and what didn't work in the past. By analyzing this, you will be able to make better decisions and set up the important tasks and processes to achieve the goal that you've set for your project. This means the fear that forecasts may be inaccurate will be reduced significantly.

Further, Kanban provides a way for the customer, client, or superior to predict that the completion time for a project is always guaranteed when you are managing it. And when this happens, it'll help build the trust and faith that they have toward letting you have control over future projects.

- **Team capacity is strengthened**

  Traditionally, when teams are tasked to do projects, they do the planning right away. But the planning ends up being more like stacking the tasks and getting them done in no particular order. However, the problem with this is that the team may face difficulties trying to get things done because they'll go beyond the capacity that they are capable of in a given time.

  That's why when Kanban is used, it shifts a team's mindset to where they're able to add more ordered tasks to the workflow, but only when they're able to do it. Plus, with the WIP limits set, the team will know that they have limits, and when they've reached them, they'll be able to keep themselves from adding more until they've completed what they've already set out to do in the first place.

- **You will improve collaboration within your team**

  Project management doesn't mean you have to do it all alone: You also have the rest of your team to help you out on what will work best. Traditional methods usually don't put much work in on collaborating because, as long as the tasks and objectives are assigned, there's nothing much else to communicate about. But with Kanban, the advantage of improved collaboration is a guaranteed.

  This means no one is left behind anymore in the team. Everyone has a role and every member, including you, can contribute. That means the processes, solutions, tasks, and opinions can all be shared. It can also establish a way for the team to brainstorm their way to victory.

Disadvantages

While Kanban is promising with all the advantages you've just learned about, there are some disadvantages you must know as well. These include:

- **Variability still exists**

  Kanban doesn't take the variability out of the picture completely. This means that the flow and the way your system is working with the project may cause confusion, mixed signals, and low-quality results. So, if a customer's needs don't match what you already set to do or unexpected factors come in, the objective you're aiming for may end up becoming different from what you originally thought in the first place.

- **Issues may arise with sudden changes**

  Another disadvantage when using Kanban is that issues may happen with sudden changes in supply and demand. This is because Kanban is best used with projects that have singular goals that are stable and repetitive. While flexibility is also an advantage, there may be times when unexpected and fluctuating changes will bring about consequences that the Kanban system isn't built for.

- **Quality mishaps may occur**

  Because variability still exists, quality can be affected too. Yes, Kanban is the system that will help you manage your inventory and get things accomplished, but quality isn't factored in for this one. What if one product needs a little redesign? What if a few items on the shelves have to be looked at one more time before they're sent out for delivery? These little factors aren't standard for Kanban, so expect quality mishaps.

- **Production flow processes might get mixed up in other areas**

  Another disadvantage when using Kanban is the various production flow processes in a company will have mixed results. While Kanban is well-suited for singular teams, having multiple teams with different tasks, product types, and goals won't exactly work very well. This can result in the company getting more downs than ups when trying to manage their productions.

- **Not having traditional time tracking habits may cause confusion**

  A misconception you'll learn about below is that Kanban doesn't allow you to track time on the tasks you'll be doing. In reality, you do track time, but just not traditionally. This can lead to confusion because most of the time, project management always involved tracking time. That's why it'll be a disadvantage to use Kanban if you're used to the ordinary way of tracking time.

Misconceptions Of Kanban

Aside from the advantages and disadvantages you've just learned about, Kanban also has its fair share of misconceptions. It's good to know them so that you'll have a better grasp on what you're planning to adapt to the projects you're managing as you go along.

- **Kanban is just a board with tasks on it**

  Kanban is mostly known for using a board and task cards as visual signals on the many processes and objectives to get a project done. This has many people think it's just that: A board. But what they aren't aware of is that Kanban isn't just a board, it's a part of a bigger structure that includes the principles, habits, and other concepts that make it a method that has been used in many industries and areas of life for decades.

  Kanban is also a method that helps you visualize the workflow that will guide you toward the completion of a project and collaborate with the rest of the team you'll be working with to cooperate so that, ultimately, success will be right in the palm of your hands.

- **Kanban is best used for support**

  When people look at Kanban, they think it's only good for support. To put it another way, they don't see other uses for it. But this is a misconception because, as you learned earlier, Toyota used Kanban for decades to get the flow of their production back into full swing. This shows that it's not just for support, its system is flexible enough to adapt to help with managing almost all projects across all industries. Whether it's producing cars or developing software, the Kanban method is almost global in scale.

- **Kanban is more suited for small teams**

  A common misconception about Kanban is that it's only well-suited from small teams because of its simple concept of visualizing the workflow and scheduling tasks. In reality, it works with big teams too.

  Large manufacturing companies have been known to adapt the Kanban method to suit their workflow very well, which is a surprise to some people. Further, the Kanban method isn't just for small and large teams; a single person such as yourself can make good use of it too.

- **Kanban is a ready-for-use method**

  Many believe Kanban is a ready-to-use method, but this is a misconception because, on its own, it's nothing. To make Kanban useful, you'll need to take its concepts, ideas, and principles and adapt them to your project. You'll also need to get your team involved so they will know what must be done to complete projects when implementing the Kanban method. So, in short, Kanban is pointless unless you have it fit into some project management system already set by you.

- **Kanban cannot be used for long-term plans**

  Most people think Kanban isn't used for long-term plans because many companies have been using it for production support that doesn't need much in the long-term. However, this is a misconception because they do in fact have long-term planning factors in motion.

Though these companies use Kanban in different ways, the one common thing they all do is set up cycles that help them be more agile and efficient in their production. This, in turn, gives them the opportunity to get the data that will finally help them establish their long-term plans to keep their production process flowing smoothly and without fail.

This also gives companies the strength to forecast their goals. Of course, they have to be very careful about how they use the data since Kanban is more about results than anything else.

- **Kanban is just for improving your process, not a workflow method**

As people look further into the Kanban method, one thing they think most of the time is that it's just for improving the process of things. But what they're not aware of is that it's also a workflow method.

The Kanban board is the keystone of the Kanban method because it's what will help you visualize the workflow and assign processes and tasks to get things done.

- **Kanban is only applied for linear processes**

Kanban is believed to be used as a tool for linear processes, where the project has a start and an end without any changes in-between. But in reality, Kanban is also used for other processes that fluctuate in the middle. This is because projects, by their very nature, aren't always linear.

There may be times that one process needs to be broken down into small parts while other processes need to be categorized into the right groups before they're able to be completed. With Kanban, you can apply the principles and concepts to all processes and get them organized in a way that will help you declutter the chaos.

- **Kanban's limits leave no flexibility**

Another misconception many people believe about Kanban is the limits included with it leave no flexibility. But this, ironically enough, actually grants flexibility because with the WIP limits implemented, you'll be able to choose the most important tasks and leave out what won't bring much to the project. Also, the limits are a way for you to choose what processes and tasks you can do simultaneously.

- **Kanban doesn't allow you to track time on your project**

Many people believe Kanban won't let you track your time on your projects. This is because Kanban lacks the time frames that most project management methods have in their concepts and ideas. But in reality, Kanban gives you a chance to track the time on your project.

How is this possible? Through the use of the Kanban board, and setting of tasks and processes underneath their respective sections, it actually gives you a different way to track the progress. It's not exactly tracking it like you'd set some kind of timeline, it's more about labelling what needs to be done, what is being done, and what has already been done.

Also, by adding what needs to be done and what has already been done in their appropriate sections, it already shows you and your team that the project is getting done one way or another, even when there is no traditional time frame for the tasks.

- **Kanban doesn't let you have any room to breathe**

Finally, another common misconception of Kanban is that it doesn't leave any breathing room for you. With the processes and tasks already set to the board, it really looks like there's no time to take a break. But actually, Kanban does leave room for you and your team to breathe.

This is because Kanban is flexible and lets you set policies that are unique and adaptive to the project. It gives you the freedom to set a time on when to get to work and when to just relax and chill.

As you learned earlier, Kanban by itself isn't a ready-to-be-used method, which means its entire concept must be adapted and actively used to be effective. In the case of breathing room, it's important to set a policy on how you and your team can relax.

Types Of Kanban Methods

Kanban isn't just a singular method; it has different types of methods. Since Ohno's first foray into project management at Toyota with Kanban, it has had varieties sprout in the later years when it began to be used by other companies. As of today, there are two major types of Kanban being used by companies and teams worldwide.

- **Withdrawal Kanban**

  This type of Kanban is mostly focused on delivering and transporting products. It's used by large companies that deal with the inventory of raw materials and products that are made to be delivered upon completion. This one is the most basic of Kanban methods since it is the one that had got Toyota back into the game. This is where continuous delivery is a requirement and the principle of visualizing the workflow is practiced to a high degree. So, naturally, the Kanban board is used for this.

- **Production Kanban**

  This type of Kanban is based more on the WIP limits. What makes this different from Withdrawal Kanban is that the project managers can use a customized Kanban task card, where they list the parts of a task that need to be focused on along with the time it takes to complete them. This is mainly used by large companies that aim to gain more efficiency with their manufacturing process.

Aside from these two types, there are four other types not commonly used, but still identified in the world of Kanban.

- **Through Kanban**

  This Kanban system is composed of the two major methods, Production and Withdrawal Kanban. This means the way the methods work individually are combined, so it speeds up the production process significantly. This also saves time when parts of the workflow can be saved for later usage. In a way, it's the best of both worlds.

- **Express Kanban**

This Kanban system, which is also called Signal Kanban, is used when a shortage of parts occurs. It's when a company identifies a need to increase what is required. The goal with using Express Kanban is to keep the production going while resupplying the parts needed.

- **Supplier Kanban**

This Kanban system involves the supplier, not the manufacturer. Since a company buys parts and other requirements through a supplier, the supplier must also keep inventory. That's why this Kanban system is modified for the supplier to use.

- **Emergency Kanban**

This type of Kanban is used for dealing with the replacement of parts that are found to be defective. It indicates sudden changes in the production of a product. To put it simply, it's the Kanban system that is used as a backup. This is the reason it's called Emergency Kanban: It's only for emergencies. It may not be a common system to use but, at the very least, it'll have companies ready for anything.

CHAPTER 3:
THE KANBAN METHODOLOGY

From its initial beginnings in 1940 to today, Kanban has evolved quite a bit. It's gotten to a point where it now has its own methodology and has been implemented in various ways. It can seem odd that this method, which was mostly known for being used in manufacturing processes, can now be used for other projects. Even the common concepts that were once exclusive to just car production factories have now been adapted to become more useful in other areas.

Common Mistakes To Avoid

As you begin to learn and apply the Kanban methodology to your projects, it's a good idea to know some of the mistakes you'll need to avoid.

- **Not fully explaining why you'll implement Kanban in the first place**

  A common mistake you should avoid is not explaining why Kanban will be used for a project. If you're only going to use it just because it's new and has some interesting things for you to try, it's not going to get you anywhere close to your goals. So, it's best to read about Kanban along with its methodology, how it compares to other systems, and see how it works with your project.

- **Not implementing work-in-progress (WIP) limits**

  Another mistake to avoid is not implementing WIP limits. This is because WIP limits are what help you set boundaries on the tasks that can be done by you and your team. It can also be a way to show you a clear view on what you're trying to achieve. Without WIP limits, it'll be difficult to even know if you're close to completion in a project.

- **Hiding things**

  This is a common mistake to avoid because if you're hiding certain things on your Kanban board, it may cause confusion. How can some of the people working on your project know what to do when they didn't see a certain activity? How can you implement WIP limits effectively if you're hiding major tasks that can help you and your team? To avoid this mistake, be a good sport and keep things visible.

- **Letting your Kanban board get cluttered**

  When you're implementing Kanban, it's a good idea to keep your board organized and clean. A common mistake to avoid is going overboard on goals and letting your Kanban board get cluttered.

  Why is this a mistake? Because if some of your staff members see disorganized task cards everywhere, it may cause confusion on what has to be done. Or, if you're doing a project yourself, you might find yourself confused as to why some of the cards you added are even there in the first place.

Here's how a cluttered board would look:

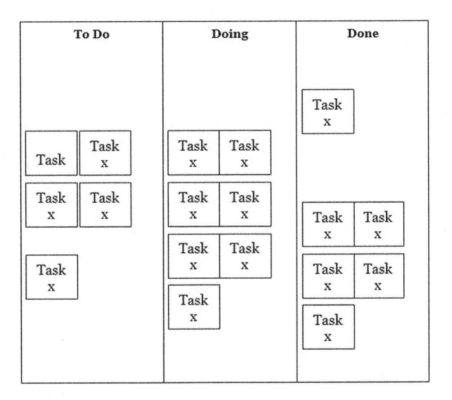

As the example shows, it's not really clear what has to be done and what has already been done. Are there some tasks that you or your team don't know about? Are some processes not set with boundaries? It can cause havoc when the workflow isn't arranged nicely.

Now here's how an organized board would appear:

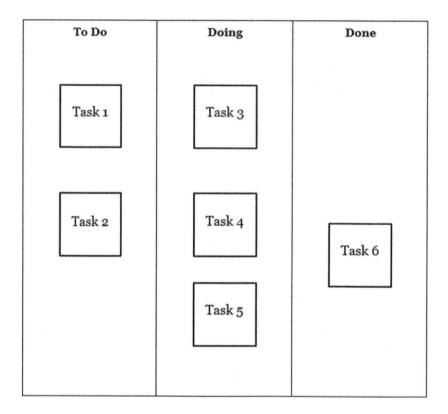

The second example shows that the tasks assigned to complete the project have been lessened and are placed in a way that tells you where the progress is right now.

So, avoid this mistake by sticking with creating a board resembling the second image.

Tips And Tricks For Kanban

Now that you're aware of the common mistakes to steer clear of, it's time to learn some tips and tricks for Kanban.

- **Pick the Kanban method that suits you**

  A good tip to remember is knowing the type of Kanban method that suits you the most. As you've learned, there are a few different types of Kanban, so review which one you like best and go for it. You can also try a combination of them if you feel that different types suit you in different ways.

- **Decide the area where you'll be putting the Kanban board**

  When you're going to use the Kanban board, it's important to have an idea on where it'll be set up. Will it be in your personal office? A common room? A meeting room? The lunch room? Pick the area and stick with it for the duration of your project. You can also have a backup plan in case the area you're aiming for isn't available in consistently throughout your project.

- **Settle on the style of the Kanban board you'll use for the project**

  When you have the area in mind, it's time to get settled on the style of your Kanban board. Will it be done in physical form? Digital form? A mix of both? By having the style decided early on, you'll be able to make the management of your tasks and workflow more efficient and effective because you'll be able to get your project managed and completed at a faster pace. Don't worry about deciding this now, the next chapter will help you choose which is best for you.

- **Discuss and set up tasks, workflows, and objectives with your team**

  Before you begin with Kanban, it's important to set up everything that needs to be done with your team. As you have already learned, a common mistake to avoid is not fully explaining why the Kanban system will be used. So, in this case, lay out everything so that when you get started, everyone knows what needs to be done.

- **Slowly adapt what you know already with the Kanban method**

  When you are implementing the Kanban method, you don't need to scrap what you already know about project management prior to this. Instead, you can adapt your stock knowledge and integrate it with what you'll learn in Kanban.

  It won't be obvious at first, but once you swap certain functions and processes and collect data, eventually the benefits will be imminent, and it'll give you a better way to manage your projects.

- **Encourage equality and leadership with everyone**

  Kanban will definitely require you to set up a hierarchy among you and your team, but that doesn't mean the hierarchy has to be traditional. This means you should practice equality and leadership with everyone on your team.

With Kanban, there's no longer a need to keep things exclusive on certain levels, because everyone can share their opinion and contribute in a way that will push the project toward completion at a much faster pace.

- **Go with the flow**

When you're implementing Kanban, you'll be seeing changes at an even pace, meaning you won't see them all at once. In this case, go with the pace and accept the changes as they come. Eventually, you'll see that it will bring positive effects to your project management method and help you complete what needs to be done with less struggles.

CHAPTER 4:

THE KANBAN BOARD

One of the common things you'll be going back to a lot is the Kanban board. First shown as one of the five core principles of Kanban in Chapter 1, the Kanban board is where you'll be charting out the various aspects of the project you're managing. You can see it as the blackboard where you'll chart everything. Except in this case, you'll be putting what you want to manage on task cards.

Here is what the typical Kanban board looks like:

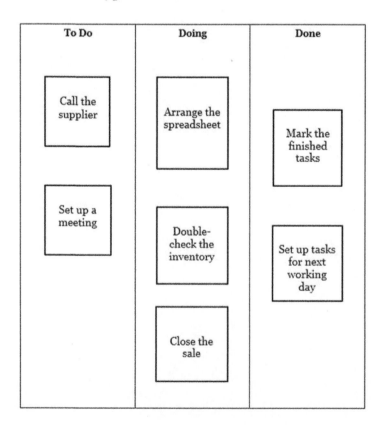

It can be confusing to look at since you're still learning how Kanban works, but you'll eventually see why it's like this. And it can be surprising when you realize this simple board is what Toyota has used for several decades to become one of the world's best automotive companies. Awesome, right?

The Kanban board can vary depending on the project that will be assigned to it, but its main template consists of three areas:

- **To Do**

  This area is where you'll assign tasks and processes that you'll be doing. They're not yet set in motion, so you can think of them as the tasks that are ready to be assigned and started.

- **Doing**

  This area is where the tasks you got from the "To Do" section are put and shows where you're making progress. This is where the majority of progress is seen because it shows that the project is moving along.

- **Done**

  This area is where the tasks you've completed under the "Doing" section are placed. This section indicates the particular tasks are done. This is a motivational section, as it shows that the project is getting closer to completion with even finished task.

With these areas, it can open up a host of variations that can be unique for each and every team. It's also a good way to see that a project doesn't have to be daunting to start with. It can finally be broken down into manageable phases that will lead to completion.

Setting Up The Board

So, how should you go about making your Kanban board? Here are the steps to follow along with images to show you how it'll look on your end:

1. **Set up the board**

   When setting up the board, have an idea on how you want it to look. If you want to make it look fancy, go for it. Or, if you're more into a simpler look, you can just make it following the examples you've already seen in the book so far, which is:

To Do	Doing	Done

2. **Arrange the materials you'll need for promptly adding tasks and processes**

   Next, gather the materials you'll need when you're ready to add the tasks and processes for your project. In this case, sticky notes are a good material to use as task cards when adding what you need on the board. You may also cut papers into small squares and use tape to stick them to the board so that when one task is done, you can remove them easily.

3. Take a look at the project and start writing out the scenario, tasks, and processes

Once you've got your board and materials ready, take a good look at the project you'll be doing. Will it be only be done by you? Or will you have a team assigned to you? Are there only two people involved? Or a hundred? Are the tasks and processes doable by the people involved? Write it all out so you have a clear picture of how the project will play out.

4. Set the WIP Limits

Next, set the WIP limits so that any ongoing tasks that are under the "Doing" section of the board won't be too overwhelming to look at. It's also a way to respect the fact that, as there are tasks that have been completed, there are also tasks that need to be done.

5. Set the policy on the tasks you'll be tackling

When setting up the tasks to be done, it's a good idea to set a policy on what can be tackled. For example, if you're with a team, you can have a policy that if a team member is too overwhelmed to tackle another task while doing their current one, they can pass on it and stay focused on their current task.

6. Map them all out with the materials you've gathered

When everything with policies, tasks, and processes is settled, you can map them all out with the materials you've gathered. This means you can pencil in the tasks on your task cards and put them in the appropriate sections on your board.

7. Get to work

So, what happens after you've set up everything on the board? You can finally get to work. This is where you'll focus on what tasks you can do, see where the progress is with the ongoing ones, and place what you've finished to finally make progress on your project.

Easy, right? But if you're not in the mood to make the board from scratch, you can check the Notes section of this book for a few templates outlined for you. You can also check out some digital programs and apps that can help you set up Kanban boards.

Digital or Physical Board?

Since Kanban was created back in 1940, the Kanban board largely consisted of a physical board and task cards. But these days, the Kanban board has its own digital form. In fact, many programs are using the digital form exclusively now.

But what form of the board should you go for? Here are things to consider when choosing your preferred from:

Digital Board

The digital board of Kanban is where you'll get your data through a computer screen or a device. This one is a common way of using a Kanban board these days. And there are many good reasons why it's the one to go for when getting started with Kanban. Here's why:

Pros:

- **The digital board can be maintained and updated at all times**

  One of the upsides of having a digital board is that it can be updated at all times. This is a big benefit, because if sudden changes or unexpected circumstances influence what you plotted out earlier, the digital board will allow you the ease of making the update at a moment's notice.

- **The digital board can be accessed anywhere**

  Another benefit of having a digital board is that it can be accessed anywhere. Whether it's from your computer or your phone, all you need to do is log in to where you saved the board and you can update it no matter where you are. You can also digitally store your Kanban task cards containing the tasks you've set up for the project so that when you need to add them to your board while you're out and about, you can do so as long as you have an internet connection.

- **A variety of programs can help you set up the digital board with just a few clicks**

   You can make a digital board instantly with programs that are available online. From Trello to Kanban Tool (discussed in the Notes section), these programs are designed to let you create a digital board without any hassles. They also have other features that many traditional Kanban boards don't have, such as real-time updates, cloud-based storage, customization tools, and more. You can even make use of Microsoft Excel if you're the type of person who likes to do things manually.

- **It can give an overview on the levels, tasks, processes, and other vital information instantly**

   Aside from the updates, the digital board has the feature of giving a complete overview of the project. From knowing who finished the first task to seeing what is an ongoing goal, the digital board is always ready for viewing. Even when you're tackling a project on your own, you can still see what needs to be done, what to do next, and what is already done.

- **The digital board can automatically organize the data you're collecting for later viewing**

   With the digital board, you can finally get a look at the data you'll need when setting up what needs to be done for your project. This is a big benefit because you have to remember that for so long Kanban boards were physical, so data collection had to be tediously done and organized on paper. But with the digital board, what took months to organize can now take as little as an hour.

- **There's more security and safety with the digital board**

  One of the things you have to remember with the physical board is there's always a chance it can be wrecked, misplaced, or misused. But with a digital board, the chances of it being destroyed or not properly used become slim because it can be stored in a cloud storage with a password.

Cons:

- **Digital boards require a mobile device or a computer to be viewed on**

  Digital boards are good and all, but the downside is that they require a device or a computer screen to be viewed. What this means is that if you're the type who likes things a bit more traditional, you may find it will be a hassle. Or, maybe you'll happily work with a digital board form, but how about some of your team members? What if they don't have the necessary devices needed for viewing it?

- **It's not of much use when there's no internet connection and no offline version set up**

  Another downside with the digital board is that it's useless when there's no internet connection and you haven't set up an offline version. What if the internet connection you have cuts out suddenly? You would go for the offline version, but what if you didn't set one up?

With our dependence on being online all the time, we forget to make an offline backup of things. You always have to be prepared because otherwise, the digital board you were so dependent on won't be accessible until you find a way to get an internet connection, stalling the progress of your project.

- **It may cause some issues with the overall principles that have already been set up prior to making the boards**

The digital board may be useful, but it may cause issues with the principles you've already set up prior to making a digital board. One example is when you and your team communicate with each other. With a physical board, you're able to talk and comment in person, so there's a social element to it. But with a digital board, it's easy to just view the screen and make comments but then there won't be any physical interaction, and this could cause misinterpretations as to the context of the comments.

Then there's the fact that a digital board may also tempt you to add more and more tasks without any prioritization, so it may lead to the consequence of not getting anything done in the long run.

- **It can be intimidating when you don't have an overall idea on how you'll map out your tasks and processes**

  The digital board may be easy to set up, but if you don't have an idea of how you'll do your tasks and processes right from the start, the features won't be of much use. As you already know, it's a misconception to think that Kanban is a ready-for-use method, so it's best you already have an idea of what your project is and how it'll benefit from Kanban.

- **There are too many features that aren't really needed**

  While the digital boards have some cool features for you to use, there is a big chance you won't really need them. In fact, many of these features are only used when you want to get really deep into the heart of the project you're working on.

  It gets to the point where the essence of Kanban is lost because you're just stuck with features that aren't really going to be relevant for you in the long run. That's why some programs that use Kanban are beginning to strip away much of these features and are sticking with the essentials, much like the Kanban board of the yesteryears.

Physical Board

The physical board used in the Kanban method is the standard, old school way of practicing Kanban. While it's not used much these days, you can still practice the method with this board form. It's a matter of knowing the benefits and risks if you go for this one.

Pros:

- **The physical board doesn't require an internet connection**

    With a physical Kanban board, you won't need an internet connection anymore. This is the old school way of setting up the board and has been the standard since back in the 1940s and 1950s. Even when the power is out or when your devices are out of power, the physical board is ready for use.

- **It uses physical materials that encourage social interaction**

    Another good thing about the physical board is it lets you use materials, such as sticky notes and magnets, to stick up the tasks you'd like everyone to know about and complete, encouraging social interaction. This makes for a rich experience because by letting the team know what's up and coming for the project, it gives a sense of camaraderie. It also allows for more collaboration. And what happens after doing this for a while? It boosts the morale in the team.

- **There is more customization involved**

    While the digital board has customization that can outperform the physical board, the latter has more customization involved because it's much more personal.

The digital board can be done on your own and without much input, but with a physical board you can really give it that much-needed boost of a personality. Also, it feels good to customize the board that hosts the project you're managing and gives you a sense of pride.

- **The dynamic changes are more effective**

The Kanban board is designed to help you pursue changes that will get you to project completion, so it goes without saying the effects you'll get when using the physical form are more effective than the digital form. This is because when you see what you've completed right in front of you, you get that feeling that you're close to completion. It just feels good. Think about it: Doesn't it feel good when you complete a task on a to-do list and add a check mark that represents that a job is done? That's how effective a physical board can be.

- **The pride and joy of making one is just special**

There's nothing quite like making a Kanban board with your own hands. When you make it, go through the Kanban method with it, and finally complete a project, there's a sense of pride that gives you the feeling of being able to achieve anything after putting in the work. That's special, right? You don't get the same kind of feeling with digital boards.

Cons:

- **Expanding the physical board is difficult**

  While the physical board is more customizable than the digital board, expanding it isn't easy. You might need to buy additional materials that will cost you a bit more than a digital board. You may also need to change the set up and re-map everything you did, especially when changes occur out of nowhere.

- **Accidents may wreck the physical board**

  Another thing to consider with the physical board is that it's not indestructible. This means accidents can wreck them and stall progress on your project. Fire, water, physical abuse; all kinds of accidents can deem the physical board useless if not taken care of properly. So, it's best to have a plan to keep your physical board from being wrecked, like a safe storage space to place the board after use.

- **Maintenance of a physical board isn't cheap in the long run**

  It may not seem like much, but when you have to replace materials, fix some parts that are making tasks unreadable, or spend money on things that will keep the board spick and span, it won't be long before you see that the cost is more than the initial set-up.

- **The context on tasks and processes might not be enough**

  Whereas the digital board already has everything you need to know about the project accessible with a few clicks, the physical board only has the visuals without much information. For example, when you see that a task under the "To Do" section is moved to "Doing," does it tell you much? There's not much meaning since all you see are the task cards. So, unless you've set up policies and processes to help you understand what the changes mean, the physical board will only be a showcase of task cards without any meaning.

- **The distribution can be tricky**

  When you're using a physical board with a team, it works well when the members are physically present to see how it looks. But then there will come a time when the members have to go home or they have to move to a different location, so the physical board won't be physically visible to them. How can you make the changes known when some of your team members might be as far away as another country? Then there's the fact that the physical board isn't good for travelling with, so you may have to leave it behind somewhere.

- **Data collection is a tedious task**

  Physical boards are nice to have and look at, but then what happens when you have to make a new one? You'll need to collect the data and store it in a way that can be viewed later. The problem is that it'll be a tedious task since you'll have to collect a large amount of data and organize it. You may skip this task but what if you need data used on a previous project for certain aspects of the current project? What if you're asked to make comparisons of how a project went from last year to this year?

- **The security is varied**

  This isn't to say that someone will try to steal it, but what if the security of the physical board you've made is varied? In many ways, the physical board you've made might be accidentally used in ways that can ruin the progress you've made.

Whichever form you choose, you'll still be able to practice Kanban. It's a matter of knowing the ins and outs of the form you've chosen and how you'll be able to adapt it with the project you'll manage.

Kanban Board Do's And Don'ts

When you're setting up the Kanban board, it's important to know some of the do's and don'ts. Whether you're going for the digital or physical form, the principles of making the board apply to both.

- **Begin with a simple form and adapt it to changes as you go along**

  When you're making the board, go with a simple form first. So, start with the three principle areas and work your way up from there. Then, as you learn to work with the board, you can start adding other sections that work well with the project. What matters most is starting with the tasks you've put on your cards so that your project is getting somewhere.

Once you're getting into the flow, you can then adapt to the changes that occur during the project. When working with a team, let them know why you'll start the project this way and adjust it so that when they see the changes, they'll be ready to tackle the tasks ahead with a strong and steady workflow.

- **Come up with unique policies**

  While you are encouraged to set up policies right from the get-go when setting up the board, it's also good to add additional policies that are unique to the project you're managing. There might be a time that the policies you need are only relevant for the current project but set them in place anyway. It'll help in the long run.

  It can also help customizing the WIP limits you'll set. For example, you can set a limit of five task cards present in the "Doing" section of the board. When two or three task cards are cleared, you can add two or three more task cards from "To Do" section. This will show that the project is flowing smoothly as more tasks are getting done.

- **Encourage feedback and inquiries**

  When you're using the Kanban board, it's good to have feedback and inquiries on the tasks and processes laid out in front of you. This can help you make the board livelier because it'll help you dig further into what the project is all about.

One way to go about this is to take a step back and see how the processes are doing. Is communication with the ongoing tasks clear across your team? Do you need to change the WIP limits? Is it better to have the "Done" section of your board have more task cards than the other sections? Having all these considerations will give you more insight on what needs to be done to make the Kanban board better than ever.

- **Don't overcomplicate the board**

  When you're making your Kanban board, it's best to not complicate it. While you are free to add some sections that may help based on the project you're working on, putting too much on the board can hamper your progress with the project.

  Whether you're on your own or with a team, it'll be overwhelming when you see that just a few days ago, the board just had a simple set of tasks and now it has so many tasks that you're not even sure if what you've added is still relevant to the project.

  So, when adding things to the board, be vigilant and ask how relevant the tasks are to the project. Once you're clear on it, add it. Otherwise, leave it be and concentrate on what is already right in front of you.

- **Don't oversimplify the board either**

  On the flip side, it's best not to oversimplify the Kanban board. Why? While simplicity can keep things from being overwhelming, it might make things stale and boring. It might also make you and your team frustrated because the act of doing the tasks and signaling that you're done them without much of a challenge seems like no great achievement.

So, it's a good idea to add a little spice to the board and keep things fresh. For example, you can add some new tasks that will level up the challenge when you or a team member finishes one of the ongoing tasks. Another example is giving a thorough and encouraging update on why one task can contribute significantly to the project more than others.

- **Be picky on the metrics and data that matter**

When setting up your Kanban board, it's important to be fastidious on the metrics and data that will matter most to your project. Why? Because this can provide a lot of information that may come in handy for future tasks. If you simply get metrics for the sake of it, that'll only be wasting your time. That's why it's important to stick with the essentials and go with the ones that will really matter for your project long-term.

- **Keep a good and tight security on the board**

It's a good idea to keep rigid security on your Kanban board. For physical boards, always have a storage area where it can be put in when you or your trusted teammates are not around. You'll never know if something will happen to it or someone might add something irrelevant by mistake, ruining the momentum of the project.

Digital boards are stored mostly in cloud-based storage, but it's still important to be safe with them. That means having a password set so that no one will be able to put irrelevant data on the board or steal data off the board.

- **Come up with ways to keep the board maintained with either form**

  The Kanban board holds the visualized workflow of your project, so it's important that you keep it maintained. Depending on the form, there are ways you can do this. For the physical board, you can try keeping tabs on some of the task cards that may need an update. You can also change the materials slowly so that they'll be more durable in the long run. For the digital board, it will be easier because you'll only need to tweak a few settings and have a set routine to do other tasks that will help you out, like collecting data for forecasting future projects.

- **Know the ways to distribute board information when needed**

  When you already have a Kanban board, you'll want to distribute the information on it when there's a need. What if you need copies of it to send to your team members in faraway places? How about when you're on vacation and need the board in a form that fits your devices? Be familiar with the ways in which you can distribute the board, and you're good to go.

- **Always have a backup version**

  When you're setting up the Kanban board, it's always best to have a backup version. Things can be unpredictable, so you should never depend on good fortune. Before you think to yourself that nothing is going to happen to your Kanban board, you'd better think again and back it up straight away.

The physical board can be backed up by creating a second version of it and storing it somewhere safe. You can also manually mimic the main board you have. It can be a bit tedious, but in the long run, it'll serve you well when the main board gets lost or damaged.

The digital board will be a cinch because you can store it in other digital storages. You might even consider getting your own private server and uploading it there without anyone being able to access it unless you grant them permission.

- **Don't have multiple boards right away**

When you're making a Kanban board, it's a good idea to have just one board when you're starting so that it's unified and is a signal that there is nothing else hidden. This is because if you have multiple Kanban boards right from the start, it can be confusing to know which is which and what needs to be done when.

This may also cause you and your team to be uncertain about whether or not you'll even be able to complete the project because what you thought to be the most important task is actually not important at all. So, to make matters simple, just keep one board for now.

- **Slowly add more boards when needed**

  On the flip side, when you and your team are getting used to the flow of the Kanban board, you can slowly add more boards. A good way to know if you're ready for this is if the team is expanding and you need more organization to manage the project. In this case, you can make another board that is specific to one team and still keep the main one. Remember to stick with the principles and you'll eventually be able to have multiple boards as long as they remain controlled.

- **Use the features that are relevant for the board**

  Whether you're using a physical or digital board, it's good to use the features relevant to either form. For the physical board, though it doesn't have as many features as the digital board, you can still use the traditional ways that many companies have used to keep track of the data needed. For the digital board, you can check on the many features included and classify which ones have the most impact on your project. Once you have what you need, you can disregard the other features and move along with the completion of your project.

The Kanban board might seem like an unnecessary concept, but overall, you'll find it's an important part of the Kanban system that you'll need to integrate when you adapt the method for your projects.

CHAPTER 5:
KANBAN'S APPLICATION

As you slowly learn more and more about the ways Kanban works, you'll want to know more about how it's applied in various ways. Originally known for making the production in manufacturing companies more efficient, Kanban has now evolved to a point that other areas are applying it for project management, albeit with adjustments.

Applying Kanban In Various Areas

Kanban's application has been cited in various areas over the last several decades. Listed below are three of the areas Kanban is commonly used.

Manufacturing System

As we already know Kanban was used as a way for Toyota to up their game in the manufacturing business. Since then, it has become the standard system for managing production in many manufacturing companies.

So, how does Kanban help in the manufacturing process? One way is that it is able to assist in communicating the need to resupply parts when a company has a shortage of a certain item. Another reason is Kanban is able to encourage its engineers to adapt practices that lead to better manufacturing results and expansion.

There's also the factor that Kanban is able to grant manufacturing companies the goal to reduce waste with respect to the raw materials they're working with and manage any excess inventory. With the help of the WIP limits, companies are able to minimize costs and meet their goals faster by finishing tasks and moving more quickly toward the completion of their overall project.

Manufacturing companies have also been able to make good use of the historical data that comes with Kanban. Since companies need proof that the Kanban method they've adapted will help with their inventory, they typically cite the usage of items which will help them manage their inventory moving forward.

Known as Key Performance Indicators (KPI), these metrics have been adapted for usage with Kanban so that companies can take note of what works and what doesn't work, then they can use what they've gathered to make a better strategy.

These are the main KPIs that have been used by the industry:

- **Lead time**

   This KPI is measured with the latency between the initiation and execution of a process.

- **Throughput**

   This KPI measures how many products are created on a line, machine, unit, or plant over a defined time period.

- **Cycle time**

  This KPI measures the time it would take for delivering a product or item from the time the work to make it was started.

Nonmanufacturing System

While Kanban has been used in Toyota and other manufacturing companies, it's also been applied in nonmanufacturing companies too, and mainly in business settings.

As many know, it can be tough to achieve more productivity at the office, especially with all the distractions. From meetings to emails, there's just so many things that can distract an employee from getting the job done.

Kanban has slowly gained popularity in business settings. So, how is it used? One way is implementing the WIP limit. This helps the employee pay more attention to the tasks they have at the moment instead of piling up more and more tasks on their plate. This also gives them a chance to increase their sense of focus so that they won't be overwhelmed. They'll be able to accomplish their goals and they can refrain from the temptation of switching between tasks. In this way, distraction is taken out of the picture.

Another way it helps is getting employees to plan out what tasks are to be done, the ones that are still ongoing, and the others that are already completed. This is a way for the workers to see the progress on the overall goal they've been paid to finish, increase their productivity, and save time.

When a team moves tasks to the "Done" section of the Kanban board, it helps to boost their morale because it shows that they're close to completion and they'll be motivated to keep on working.

Apart from the Kanban board and principles, businesses have also implemented other ideas that aid their application of Kanban. From timers to customized signals, the office has found ways to make the most out of the Kanban method in its own way.

Software Development

Software development might be unusual to consider when applying Kanban but, surprisingly enough, it's used quite commonly. It's what many like to cite Kanban's use for because it has actually developed a different kind of Kanban method. It's a unique method, and, in a way, a hybrid: Agile Kanban.

Agile Kanban is a concept in software development that integrates the principles of Kanban. This has become a popular approach in the world of software development because it expands upon the visualized workflow principle and maps out the tasks and other processes planned out on Kanban task cards in digital form.

What makes it different from the other project management programs that aid in software development is Agile Kanban doesn't include the time-boxed feature, much like the original Kanban. So, the continuous delivery of a product or item is encouraged with this method.

Because of the five core principles, and other profound concepts found in the original Kanban method, Agile Kanban is able to approach software development in a whole new way. This means software companies are able to meet a customer's demands with a slight change of data that can help them create a new alternative solution. It can also help the development team collaborate and provide feedback so that the tasks assigned to their project can be completed at a much faster pace.

Other Areas Kanban Has Been Applied In

Aside from the three areas that you've just learned about, Kanban has also been applied throughout other areas that you would never expect. After all, Kanban provides flexibility. However, it can be surprising to see how the areas listed below were able to apply the Kanban method.

Home

Kanban can definitely be applied at home. It can be started with just the basic Kanban board, a few task cards, and a list of the tasks that need to be finished. Another way is making a chore board with Kanban policies implemented.

For example, if you're living with your family, you can make a board that has the chores that need to be done on a weekly or daily basis listed on task cards. You can then assign the tasks to your family members. You might try it by age or by capacity. You can also get everyone to collaborate and make a rotation on how the chores will be distributed.

Another way Kanban can be used at home is applying it for inventory management on your fridge and pantry. This is applied by assigning task cards for certain items that normally run out quickly. When this happens, you can stick task cards with the listed items on the section of a customized Kanban board that informs you that need to resupply that particular item.

Events

Can Kanban be applied to events such as birthday parties and weddings? Yes, it can. A great way to do this is looking at the many tasks that will be considered when planning a party. Will the guests need to be sent the invites by a set date? Is the venue appropriate? With the Kanban system applied, it'll make event planning easier than ever. It'll also open up the line of communication between the party planners that will be handling the event.

Another way Kanban can be applied with event planning is how you can make use of the ABC classification system, which you will learn about in the subsequent chapter, to prioritize what must be done to get everything prepared for the day of the event.

Kanban Success Stories

Kanban is quite the system to use in many areas. That's why the companies listed below were able to apply the principles of Kanban successfully and gain a name for themselves. These successful companies include:

Spotify

One of the world's most popular music streaming services has found success with the Kanban method. But how? Implemented by an engineer who had an issue with scalability and wanted to find a solution for growing the company, he was able to encourage Spotify to implement the Kanban method as a way to make changes to the workflow at the time.

They started with just a simple form of the Kanban board, starting with the three principle areas: "To Do," "Doing," and "Done." They then set up WIP limits on the "To Do" and "Doing" sections of their board to indicate the boundaries of the tasks at hand. And, in time, they added a few subsections on the three main areas.

The result? Spotify's productivity and growth skyrocketed. So, it goes to show that even a company like Spotify can make a simple project management method like Kanban work to their advantage.

Blizzard Sport

This one is a surprising case. Blizzard Sport, an Austrian ski equipment manufacturer and alpine ski producer, once had a major setback when they were managing their IT operations team. They weren't quite able to keep them in check, which led to a lot of issues, such as long cycle times and frequent delays.

But thanks to the manager of the team being inspired with a book he read on Kanban, he was able to implement the method, and in no time the IT team bounced back from their shaky status.

The team used a customized version of the Kanban board that catered to their unique tasks within the company. While it was vastly different from most Kanban boards, it still helped the IT team get more things done, and soon they were able to reduce the delays, make their clients happy, and bring back a more content and productive work atmosphere. The manager even received an award for this achievement.

Seattle Children's Hospital

This hospital was having an issue of short supply on items that were important for their patients and doctors. Because of this, the nurses had to restock these items from various locations, but this way of resupplying caused many delays. This had the doctors worried that they wouldn't be able to treat their patients sufficiently because they were more stressed about getting more supplies than actually treating their patients.

So, what was the solution? A Kanban system. Using a unique system from a tool called BlueBin, Seattle Children's Hospital was able to view their data after a year and took note of what they could do to make resupplying work efficiently. In no time, the hospital began to see significant improvements in their inventory. This gave way to better habits, such as the hospital not discarding any expired goods, which saved them money.

How To Apply Kanban To Your Projects

So, with all that in mind, how can you apply Kanban to your project? How will you be able to do what the previously listed successful organizations did?

- **Remember what you learned in Chapters 1, 2, and 3**

  When you're about to apply Kanban to your projects, remember what you've learned in Chapter 1, 2, and 3. It's a good idea to know the core principles as well as the methodology, advantages, disadvantages, and other concepts by heart so that when you're starting the project, you'll know what to do without getting overwhelmed.

- **Adjust what you can accordingly**

  Not all projects are equal, so it's best to adjust accordingly when you're applying Kanban to your projects. This means you have to take note of what will work and what won't work, just like the organizations you've read about in the previous section. They made use of Kanban in a way that catered to their unique needs. Traditionalists might argue that's not how Kanban works, but then again, Kanban's principles and methods inspired those organizations to achieve success.

- **Discard parts of Kanban that you know won't work in the long run**

  When applying Kanban to your project, take note of any concepts from the method that won't work and discard them. It may feel like you're disregarding the core principles, but you're not. You are adapting it to a project that might not even be a good fit for Kanban at all. That's why when you take what works instead, you'll achieve better progress toward the completion of your projects.

- **Coordinate with the team on how Kanban can be applied**

One of the common mistakes you have to avoid is not explaining fully why Kanban is needed. So, it goes without saying that you'll need to coordinate with the team on how Kanban can be applied to the project. It can come off as a bit strange, especially when the project you're working with them on is unlikely to benefit from Kanban. But with cooperation and collaboration, you will soon see the benefits.

CHAPTER 6:
ABC CLASSIFICATION

When read somewhere else, the ABC classification can sound like a term for teaching preschoolers. But in the business world, it's actually a term for managing production, and how it applies for Kanban will surprise you quite a bit.

What Are The ABCs?

When discussing the ABC classification, you'll be considering it in terms of inventory. But don't worry, you can also consider it in other terms that you'll be applying to your unique project.

- **Class A**

  Class A items make up 20% of the inventory, which also account for 80% of the total value. These items cost the most to use, either because of their volume usage or the unit cost.

  Class A items are replenished on restrictive terms because of the high cost involved with them and the investments that are needed to maintain them. That's why the managers involved in keeping them in check have to spend most of their time ensuring they don't run out of that specific item.

  They may not have as much stock as the items listed below, but their value is quite high and is the reason they're labeled as Class A.

- **Class B**

    Class B items make up 30% of the inventory and account for 15% of the total value. Unlike the Class A items, these have a predictable pattern, have a lower impact on inventory, and need to be replenished with a fixed routine.

    These are the items that must be kept in moderate amounts since they don't have as much impact as Class A items, they're easy to monitor and control without making them too much of a burden.

- **Class C**

    Class C items make up 50% of the inventory and account for 5% of the total value. Compared to Class A and B items, Class C items have very low costs but are stocked at higher quantities.

    For these items, it's recommended to have an automation controlling stock because there's no need to put much attention into them. You can simply set a system that stocks these items automatically as necessary. Also, it's best not to worry too much about Class C items because that means you won't be giving due attention to managing Class A and B items, which have more value.

How ABC Items Can Be Adapted To Your Project

It can be confusing to read about the ABC items you've just read about since they're mostly concerned with inventory management. But it can be seen differently. You can think of these items in the way they are ranked in terms of importance and urgency.

So, a good way to go about this is adapting the concept of the ABC classification to your project is:

1. **Take a step back and understand what your project is about**

   When you're about to classify your project tasks in accordance to the ABC classification, take a step back and understand what your project is all about first. Is it about software development? Is it about office productivity? Is it about something that hasn't been tried before? This will help you understand the tasks and processes you'll be mapping out later. When you have an idea in mind, you can move to the next step.

2. **Map out the tasks and processes you'll be doing**

   Next, map out all the tasks and processes that build up the project from top to bottom. From calls to the scheduling meetings, leave nothing out. This is all about breaking down the project to bits and pieces you can manage easily. A good way to get this organized is using a pen and paper to write them all down. You can also get your phone or computer and writing them in a digital word document so that you can send it to your team to review.

3. **Consider how important each task and process are and know its impact on the overall project**

   When you have every task mapped out, you should evaluate how important they are to the project and how much impact they will make. This will give you a better view of the project in the long run. For example, is the one task you wrote down something that will make a big impact on the project as a whole? Write that down.

4. **Mark it by the ranking of the ABC classification**

   With the tasks and processes all mapped out in terms of your consideration on what you feel is important to the project, you can rank them with the ABC classification. For example, if one task covers the majority of the project and has significant value, classify it as Class A. But if it's a task that can be automated and won't need much monitoring, classify it as Class C.

5. **Organize what you've just ranked as a chart**

   Once you have everything ranked, it's time to map your tasks on a chart for easy reference. Here's how it should look:

Class A	Class B	Class C
Setting up the structure for Kanban Teaching Kanban to team	Keeping a supply of materials for the Kanban board	Make sure to keep the work environment clean Maintain proper hygiene Remember the Kanban principles

Why ABC Classification Can Be Beneficial

Though ABC classification can be a little tedious to do at first, it can actually provide benefits when used right. Here are some of them:

1. **It can help you see how important the items you have for the project are**

   A benefit of the ABC classification is that you'll be able to see how important the items for your project are. This means you'll see which ones aren't really important, so you can cross them off your list. It can also help you see that when items you deemed as Class A actually turn out to be Class B, you'll understand the project you're currently managing, as well as subsequent projects, with better perspective.

2. **It'll give you the ability to prioritize which of the items to go first**

   ABC classification is also beneficial because once you already have your items classified, you can prioritize what task to go for first, so you won't be going all over the place when you start. Plus, you'll be able to see that the item you once thought was the most important thing is just something you can put on the side until the other items under Class A are dealt with.

3. **It'll keep you organized while managing the project**

   With this classification, you'll be able to be better organized while managing the project because with the items you've already classified have given you a grasp on what has to be done. It also gives you a clear strategy on how you can see the project through to completion with the most efficiency.

4. **It'll help your team see what the priorities throughout the project are**

While it might come as a new concept to learn and understand for your team, ABC classification will be a great benefit for them because they'll be able to see what their specific priorities are throughout the project. They'll know that the items ranked in Class A and B are what they must tack while the ones in Class C can be automated and so on.

How Kanban Can Be Used For ABC Classification

In summary, the ABC classification is a way for you to see which parts of the project are important. So, it doesn't necessarily have to be about the inventory because, as you've just learned now, it can be adapted to any of your projects. This means ABC classification be applied to not just tasks but also objectives, processes, and other essential things that make the bulk of the project.

With all that in place, you'll now need to know: How can Kanban be used with ABC classification?

1. **Look up the items you've ranked under the ABC categories of your project early and determine if they're right**

So, you've ranked your items under the ABC classification before beginning your project. Now, you should give your items a good look. If your project involves a lot of inventory, this should be easy for you to do. However, if you're dealing with things that are non-tangible, you'll have to discuss this with your team.

For example, if the project involves an important office meeting, is it right to classify the task of setting up the time for it as Class A? Should getting the meeting place ready be classified as a Class B? The answers to these questions change based on the meeting, that's why it's important for you to look over the ranked items before you decide on your final list.

2. Make cards that are linked for the categories

When you have finalized your tasks based on the ABC classification, you can now get to work and set up the cards that are linked to the categories. As you already know, visual signals are an important part of Kanban, so set up cards with colors related to importance. For instance, you can set up Class A cards to be the color red to indicate they're important and must be focused on first, while Class B cards can be the color blue to indicate they're not to be worried about it too much but can still be maintained and watched over. As for Class C cards, they can be signaled with the color yellow to indicate that, while they may not have much impact, they can still be important.

3. **Map out a strategy with how you'll tackle the ABC items**

With the ABC cards all set up, you'll need a strategy on how to tackle them. A good way for you to do this is to follow what you've learned in the previous chapters. You can also make good use of the board so that while you're making progress with the project you can already see how close you are to completion.

4. **Stick with the principles**

Most importantly, it's still a good idea to stick with the principles discussed in Chapter 1. Even when you're dealing with the ABC ranking of the items on your Kanban board, you still have to be consistent and disciplined with the way you'll achieve the task at hand.

5. **Set up policies unique for the ABC items**

As you're tackling the ABC items, it's good to also have some policies set up along the way because there may be times the ABC items won't remain as they are. What if a Class A item on your board turns out to be a Class B later? What if an upcoming task is actually a Class C? By having policies beforehand, you'll be able to handle the changes in ABC items that will come and go in a good manner.

It can be tricky to get used to classifying the items you'll be assigning to your projects, but in time you'll see why it can be handy to know which of them belongs to which class. And with Kanban applied, it'll make things a whole lot easier to organize.

CHAPTER 7:

KANBAN VERSUS OTHER SYSTEMS

Kanban isn't the only system that helps you with project management, there are other systems as well. But while they may have similarities, they also have major differences. So, it's a good idea to know what makes them different from the usual systems you might come across in your journey.

Kanban Versus Traditional MRP System

The traditional MRP (material requirements planning) system is a control system that is involved with production, inventory, and scheduling. In a way, the primary goal is just the same as Kanban: To keep inventory levels low but still have enough to meet customer's needs and make a profit. But the difference is how both systems achieve the goal.

When you use the Kanban system, you're able to achieve the goal by mapping out your project on the board and scheduling the tasks based on what you'll do, what's in progress, and what's already been done with the use of cards to signal that a certain task has been done and shows the project is progressing.

As for the MRP system, you'll fulfill the objectives by forecasting demands. This means you'll make an analysis and predict how much you think customers will need certain products. If what you forecasted is right, you'll make a profit. But if it's the opposite, you lose money.

71

Looking at the ways the systems work, it's clear Kanban surpasses the MRP system because while the latter enables you to forecast, it can take time and analysis of probability to make your predictions accurate. There's also the factor of unpredictability, so it's like gambling. But with the former, you have the actual inventory on your side, and you have control over how the flow will go with supply and demand. There's also the factor of flexibility.

Kanban Versus XP

Another system to compare Kanban to is XP. XP, which stands for extreme programming, is a management system that's used in software development. For this one, the main goal is to be able to deliver great quality for the software promised to the customer. To put it another way, it's all about customer satisfaction. This one is vastly different from Kanban because it focuses heavily on what the customer wants, so a team that uses XP will base their tasks heavily on the customer.

This also encourages everyone to be very open with one another, have good communication lines, and set up policies that are a bit more extreme than what Kanban entails you to do. You can think of XP as the Kanban system with a more hands-on approach to project management.

But the downside with XP is that while it is great to have the customer's feedback as your project planning basis, it may lead to some adverse consequences, such as losing grip on the main goal of the project, not being able to finish some of the tasks that were set up initially because of the constant changes that have been made, and the tendency to switch the flow in the middle of the project when a good flow has already been established.

With the Kanban system, flexibility ensures that you can still ensure the customer's satisfaction as part of the project, but it'll also give you the freedom to establish policies that will safeguard full equality.

Kanban Versus Scrum

Finally, we have Scrum to compare with to Kanban. Scrum is a framework system that's designed to help teams work together with various processes and practices that ensure they're able to collaborate. Much like a sports team will work together to score a goal, Scrum provides the necessary tools for a team to make sure they've got what it takes to reach the goal of the project.

Unlike Kanban, Scrum is largely team-based, so this is the one system you cannot do alone. You'll need a team if you want this system to work for you. It also has processes specific for how teams can handle tasks.

For example, while Kanban lets the team know what they have to do with the help of visualization, Scrum gets the team up to speed on what you'd like them to do by dividing them into a number of sub-teams.

Another example is that with Scrum you classify the tasks with the understanding that they're ranked in a fixed way. This means that there is a larger context that can give the rest of the team a better understanding on what needs to be done on the project. As for Kanban, there can be a misunderstanding since you have to be very precise and specific on how things will be right from the start.

In many ways, Scrum can actually trump Kanban because the system is more rigid and structured, and when applied correctly, can really help in tackling projects that are too large for the Kanban system to handle.

Combining Kanban With Scrum

Kanban, by its very nature, is a system that requires you to really adapt the method to the specific project you're managing. You can't expect it to make things work for you. As for Scrum, you'll need a team, but the framework is already correct from the get-go, so it's a matter of following what has already been established.

So, it's quite a surprise to learn that Kanban can be combined with Scrum. Despite the differences, Kanban and Scrum can be used together with just a few considerations:

- **Learn the differences of the systems**

  When you're combining Kanban and Scrum, it's best to learn the differences between them. Once you have a grasp of them, you can adjust accordingly so that you won't run into any conflicts when you're slowly making the two systems work together for your project.

- **Use unique features from one system where the other system lacks**

  Both systems have their own unique features, so use those features when the other system lacks them. It can be tricky at first, but once you know which is which, you'll be able to swap and use the features swiftly without running into any issues.

- **Discuss with the team on how you'd like it to work**

  Scrum is largely a framework that encourages you to work with a team, so you'd better make sure that when you're implementing Kanban with it, you let your team know how you'd like the systems to work in tandem. It may take time, but they'll eventually understand how it'll benefit the project they're working on.

- **Take the best of both systems and integrate them into your own personal system**

  As you learn to make things work with Kanban and Scrum, try to take the best of both worlds and slowly integrate them so that you can finally have your own personal system to work with. This has been done by many different organizations. Some software development teams work with a version called Scrumban which takes the many concepts of Kanban and combines them with Scrum to make a framework that resembles Kanban but still functions as Scrum. Scrumban may not work for you, but there's a benefit to integrating the two distinct systems that have similar methods to achieve the same goal.

CHAPTER 8:

SCALING

One thing many go for when they use Kanban in managing their projects is scaling. This is where they'll handle the growth of a project in a cost-effective manner. Another way to put it is that it's a matter of expanding the projects you're managing through various sizes while still keeping costs to the minimum. After all, if the project feels too insignificant, wouldn't it be nice to make it bigger and see the possibilities?

Difficulties

Before diving into the scaling possibilities, it's best to know that there are difficulties to be found. It may look promising, but in reality, what you'll be facing isn't as easy as you think.

- **Misunderstandings are bound to happen**

  When you attempt to scale with Kanban, you'll find misunderstandings will occur. For example, when you decide to increase the scale of one aspect on the board, you may be sending mixed signals to other team members because they might not know why that aspect deserves to be scaled above others.

  Another example is when you try to scale an aspect of the project when it's not yet the right time. This will get the rest of the team disoriented because they're already committed to their assigned tasks but will find what they've been doing isn't relevant or significant anymore.

- **You may go over the limits**

  It can feel great to make scaling work when using Kanban but there is a temptation to go overboard. How so? You might find that the scale you'll initially go for may feel too small, so you'll try and experiment by making it bigger. But then it still may not satisfy you, so you'll make it even bigger. Then as the cycle goes, you'll find the limits you accepted at the beginning of the project no longer exist, and the scale just keeps getting bigger until the boundaries are gone. You'll then find your project doesn't have a clear purpose anymore.

- **You may get overwhelmed with the sheer size you've just created**

  One difficulty you'll want to understand is the overwhelming impact you'll get with the sheer size you've created by scaling. When it's not fully controlled, you'll find the scale will be too big for you to handle. In fact, you might find yourself putting so much on your plate that you can't even keep anything organized anymore. You may even end up committing the common and disastrous mistake of having a cluttered Kanban board.

- **The disadvantages of Kanban will likely unfold**

  Another difficulty you'll be faced with when scaling is that the disadvantages associated with Kanban, described in Chapter 2, will likely occur on your end. This can mean everything from poor-quality results to the variability factor causing production processes to falter.

- **Project completion will take longer than usual, or not happen at all**

  Though scaling can be a good thing, another difficulty to take note of is project completion will take longer than usual. This is because what started out simple will be a bit more complicated as more tasks and processes are added to the workflow. Plus, it may be a bit of a drag for the rest of the team when they find what they already finished before the scaling process is only just a small part toward completing the project. Also, if you go overboard with scaling and incur the negative effects of Kanban, your project might fail altogether.

How To Make Scaling Work With Kanban

While scaling is difficult, it can still work with Kanban. It's a matter of knowing the right way to go about it. It can take time, but you'll be able to pull it off. Here are some ways to get you started:

- **Consider why you will be scaling in the first place**

  An important thing to consider before scaling with Kanban is why you'll do it in the first place. Reflect on your choice and find out why. You can list out the pros and cons and see how it'll go. This will give you a chance to see where it will take the progress of your project before you make a decision. You can also let the team know about your decision to scale and give them an idea of where it will take them as the project progresses.

- **Set levels within your team**

  When doing your best to make scaling work with Kanban, try to assign levels in your team. For example, you can ask someone to watch over a certain level of tasks while you overlook the whole horizon. Another example is assigning two or three members to manage the workflow while another two or three execute the tasks at hand. It's all about giving members a clear sign of their duties and the impact they will have on the project.

- **Assign leaders**

  Another good way to make scaling work is assigning leaders. While you are the top leader, you need lower level leaders within your team who can help you out when you're dealing with bigger things. So, when you have the project levels set up, pick leaders for them and let them know what their tasks will be to keep everything running smoothly.

- **Implement a system for your policies**

  Because scaling will involve you expanding, it's a good idea to have a system set up for policies you'll need to implement. This means when something needs to be addressed or when a new task comes along, the policies that set up within a system can be used and the new tasks won't further delay your project.

- **Maintain the five principles of Kanban with the board**

  Make sure to maintain discipline with the Kanban board. Even when you're building up to bigger things you didn't think were possible, you still have to keep the principles and disciplines of the method intact. Even when new tasks and processes are added, you must remember to never lose sight of why you're doing this.

- **Stick with the agreed scale**

  When you're maintaining discipline, it's important to agree with the scale you've settled on. This means that no matter what, the scale will never go beyond what was set in place. Even when the rewards look promising, you have to stick with the agreed scale. It may not look beneficial, but in the long run you'll see that staying with what you committed to will pay off.

- **Understand the ownership factor**

  Another thing you can do to make scaling work with Kanban is understanding the ownership factor and how it works. Remember when you set levels and assigned leaders? You can now give the ownership to those who will handle the tasks and the workflow. This will not only give better focus, but it'll also show that you and your team members understand what your respective responsibilities are and how to do things to achieve what is necessary.

- **Be familiar with the two types of scaling as you go along**

When you're slowly getting into scaling with Kanban, it's also important to know the two types of scaling you can perform. First, there's breadth scaling, which means you'll be adding downstream and upstream areas in your system. This is also where you'll add more value with what you're doing. A good way to see it is that as you begin to expand, you can integrate what is valuable to the project and let the rest of the team know that there is a benefit to it.

Then there's the depth scaling, which is where you'll make the Kanban system you're using grow to a deeper level. This doesn't mean you'll suddenly have the freedom to overcomplicate it. It's more about seeing the system evolve to a point that you'll be adding other tools that will come in handy as you move along with the project.

- **Maintain and track progress on the multiple boards**

As you scale your project, you may find the need to add more Kanban boards. In this case, it's best to maintain and track the progress on the boards that will be set up. This is to ensure that all parts of the project will be done and will near completion as more and more tasks are done. You must also make sure that you're maintaining the core principles and not losing sight of the overall goal.

CHAPTER 9:
CERTIFICATION

For many years, Kanban has been one of the standard systems for managing inventory and, in later years, has been applied as the system for managing projects that can help people be more organized in whatever area they're applying it in. That's why many companies want to keep the practice alive with different certifications.

The Benefits Of Getting Certified

Kanban certifications may not look like much on the surface but will bring about many opportunities for you. Here are reasons why:

1. **It'll open up job opportunities**

   With a Kanban certification, you'll be able to find many opportunities for jobs in various sectors. There might be a company that needs a Kanban expert in their department. There's bound to be a small business that wants someone with the knowledge of Kanban methodology. There may even be a well-known company abroad that'll let you test your Kanban skills to improve their company's workflow. However you go about it, one thing's for sure: The opportunities are there.

2. **It'll get you high gear in your career**

   Another benefit for getting certified is your career advancement will get a very significant boost. How so? If the company you're working for honors the Kanban method as an essential part of its workflow, you'll be able to make use of the skills you'll learn through certification and show your bosses that the projects they assign you and your team can be done effectively and efficiently.

3. **You'll be able to get advanced levels**

The Kanban certification will also help open up the path toward learning about the advanced levels of Kanban training. You can think of the certifications you'll learn about below as level 1 while the advanced levels are levels 2, 3, and above. And with the advanced level of skills you learn, it'll help you boost your skills to the max.

4. **You'll have more knowledge on how Kanban can be applied to other areas**

When you become certified, you'll have way more knowledge about Kanban. As you'll learn from the places that can give you certification in the Notes section, there are private forums where other certified professionals gather to share their tips and tricks on how to make the most out of Kanban.

5. **You can teach Kanban to others**

Two of the certifications you'll learn more about below let you learn Kanban and teach it to others. One of them gives you a chance to be a teacher while the other gives you the opportunity to be a trainer. This is a benefit because being able to share your knowledge of Kanban will no doubt boost the morale of the students you'll teach. It'll also help you keep the Kanban method alive with others.

The Recognized Kanban Certifications

When you're beginning with Kanban and wondering how you can get certified, it can be daunting to know how to get started. Don't worry, listed below are the recognized Kanban certifications worldwide. While the teaching methods are different, the main goal still remains the same.

Team Kanban Practitioner

The Team Kanban Practitioner (TKP) certification gives you the skills to help your team achieve higher levels of efficiency and collaboration. Suggested for managers, this certification is open to everyone at any experience level. This is also a great to get started with option because there are no prerequisites needed, so even if you haven't got the other certifications, you can sign up to get your TKP certification right away.

The TKP certification has four objectives for those who will sign up for this:

- Improving communication within the team they're managing and encouraging a stronger sense of collaboration.

- Being able to organize the team's workload for further progress toward project completion.

- Having the skills to manage risks and unexpected circumstances.

- Gaining better visibility on goals and objectives.

In many ways, the TKP certification is the way to go if you're eager to get your team up and running through the Kanban method with a strong start.

Kanban Coaching Professional

If you're the type who likes teaching others and want to pass on what you know about Kanban, then the Kanban Coaching Professional (KCP) certification is for you.

Considered as the highest position a Kanban coach can achieve, the KCP certification is a total evaluation of a professional's overall history in Kanban coaching. For you to get this certification, you'll need to be someone who is already a trainer, consultant, manager, or practitioner dealing with the Kanban method. This can be a challenge to obtain, but if you're eager to teach others the greatness of Kanban, you'll want to get this one.

There are also valuable points to consider when you pursue this certification, such as:

- Gaining access to forums that are only available for KCP certified individuals.

- Being able to get updates and other forms of knowledge that will provide you with new techniques associated with Kanban that you never see in the areas open to non-KCP certified individuals.

- Having the opportunity to contact coaches and clients about methods in Kanban that will help you further boost your skills.

Kanban Management Professional

The Kanban Management Professional (KMP) certification is very popular and well-known worldwide. When pursuing this one, you'll gain an understanding of making decisions that help you improve workflow in projects and skills that will assist you in giving a company the highly sought-after customer satisfaction most companies are in need of.

This certification also includes specialized training for the Kanban method that provides many benefits. Also, just like the other certifications, KMP certification has these valuable pointers:

- You're able to gain better skills in managing inventory with a better understanding on what to do when the supplies are running low.

- You'll have a better grasp on how the WIP limits can be implemented so that you'll be able to manage teams better with the tasks they've been assigned.

- You'll be able to move from one process to another without losing pace or focus. This will give you the ability to manage a project when its broken down into different parts.

86

Accredited Kanban Trainer

For the trainer who wants to teach Kanban, this one's for you. The Accredited Kanban Trainer (AKT) certification gives you the skills that are necessary when you're seeking to offer training classes that deal with the Kanban method. It also gives you the opportunity to be a trainer in organizations that deal primarily with Kanban and with clients who pay for private classes.

The certification is also valuable thanks to these benefits:

- Having more opportunities for job positions that let you be the trainer and project manager in high-value companies.

- Being able to get a team up and running with confidence and power.

- Getting the skills to handle all types of Kanban methods and knowing which of them to implement on different projects.

Another great thing about this certification is that it gives you access to other resources that most certified individuals can't get, making it very attractive if you're the kind of person who likes having high-level knowledge on any subject matter.

Boosting Your Skills With Certifications

Once you obtain the certifications, they won't be much of use if you're not going to take advantage of the skills you'll gain from them. But how will you do that? Here are a few ways:

1. **Take advantage of what the certification classes will offer you**

When boosting your skills, it's a good idea to take advantage of what the certifications hold for you. They all vary in accordance to what they're designed for, so keep that in mind. This means if the certification grants you skills in managing a team, then take advantage of that. But if you're the type of person that takes on projects alone, you should go for certifications that are designed for managers.

2. **Apply and practice what you have learned in the projects you're managing**

When you've gained a certification, you should apply what you've learned to the projects you're currently managing. This will strengthen your skills because you're now able to practice what your classes have taught you, and practicing theoretical knowledge is always the way to go when you want to improve your skills.

3. **Be creative on how you can apply your skills with areas you feel need Kanban**

Another way you can strengthen your skills is being able to come up with ways to apply those skills in areas you feel need Kanban. This can bring a lot of value to your life, because even the most unlikely of areas can be successful with Kanban. It can boost your skills because applying your knowledge tests just how much you understand of the Kanban methodology.

4. **See how you can combine it with other project management methods**

When you have a certification and are eager to improve your skills, why don't you try combining it with other systems? As you learned in Chapter 7, Kanban can be combined with Scrum, and with the skills you've learned while getting certified, you'll have a better idea of how to do that. This can better your understanding of the method because it will help you see how well Kanban can be adapted to other method's features.

CHAPTER 10:
PRACTICING KANBAN SOLO

The Kanban method has largely been used for teams, which often makes people wonder: Can you practice Kanban all on your own? Yes, you can. It's just a matter of tweaking a few things that you've learned about.

Reasons Why You Might Try Practicing Kanban Alone

There's no shame in admitting that you prefer to work alone rather than on a team. This is probably what lead you to question if Kanban can be practiced alone in the first place. But why go solo with Kanban when it was meant for teams? Here are a few reasons:

1. **You're just starting out on a project**

   One reason you might be trying to practice Kanban alone is you're just starting out on projects all on your own. You're just getting used to what Kanban is all about and want to try it and see how everything goes when you're managing your projects.

2. **You'd like to get your life more organized**

   Kanban may be known for mostly being used in the manufacturing industry, but it has been applied in other areas that aren't involved with cars. It can even be a system that will help you organize your life. With its principles and methods, who wouldn't find it a good way to improve their life?

3. **You feel like the Kanban method isn't going to be a good fit with other people**

Kanban is quite the system, and it's not suited for everyone. So, naturally, you may find it won't fit well with others because a lot of the ideas aren't as familiar as other traditional project management methods, so it may cause confusion for many and you're not exactly keen to explain it fully (yet).

4. **You'd like to see how far it will take you**

Then there's the reason of being able to challenge yourself in seeing how far it'll take you. As human beings, we challenge ourselves to be better all the time. That's why practicing Kanban on your own can be the perfect way to see how capable you are of managing your projects and adapting the method your way.

How To Practice Kanban Solo

With the reasons out of the way, it's time to learn how you can adapt it solo. So, how should you go about it? Here are some ways to get started:

1. **Be vigilant on the projects you'll adapt Kanban with**

When you're doing a project on your own, be vigilant when you're adapting Kanban. This means much of what you'll be doing with the Kanban principles will be adjusting them without a team. So, be focused on knowing how you want things to work for yourself and make sure you've got it all under control.

2. Set up your own policies

When you're practicing Kanban solo, it's a good idea to set up your own policies. But the difference here is you'll have to make sure these policies are for you and no one else. This means when a certain task you've assigned is about to get done, know the self-imposed policy on how you can deal with it. If you like, you can also set the policies as a rule list that can be pinned up alongside your board as a constant reminder.

3. Make simple boards and don't spend too much on digital programs

Because you'll be working solo, it's best to stick with simpler boards. As for the digital programs listed in Notes, it's best not to spend too much money on them. You can even get started with simpler programs, such as Evernote and Microsoft Excel, to serve your needs for a digital board. As for the physical board, a pen and a piece of paper should do the trick for you.

4. Be respective of your own WIP limits

When you're setting your own WIP limits, respect them at all costs. While you are practicing Kanban solo, it's important to respect yourself and your capacity. So, this means when you've reached the WIP limit, take a pause and let yourself breathe. Don't let yourself get overwhelmed when completing the tasks for the project. You can also mark the WIP limits so when you feel like doing other tasks and see the mark, you already know what you have to do.

5. **Feel free to make the sections your own**

When you're crafting your Kanban board, you can set the sections according to your preference. This means you can name them however you like now that you're not with a team. So, you can call the "To Do" section your "Task" section, the "Doing" section as your "Ongoing Work In Progress" section, and the "Done" section "Completed" or "In Review" section. This will encourage you to be more engaged with your project.

6. **Don't overthink on all aspects of the project**

When practicing Kanban on your own, don't overthink all of your project's aspects. Kanban was designed to help you organize the tasks so that you can finish them and near the completion of your project efficiently, so it's best to know what you're aiming for and stick with your goals until the very end.

7. **Don't complicate the storage solutions you'll have with your board**

When you're backing up your board, there's no need to complicate things since you're practicing Kanban solo. This means when you're storing the board, you can do it in simple ways.

When you're working with a physical board, you can store in an area that's safe for you such as your closet or a drawer. As for the digital board, you can store it in cloud-based storages that won't be too much on your wallet. You can even use Google Drive and make use of the free 15GB that's already offered with your Google account. But if you're not much of an online person, you can use a USB drive to store your digital board so that even when there's no online connection, you already have the board ready for use.

8. Apply the principles that are only relevant to your scenario

As you've learned, the Kanban method has five core principles, but a majority of them only work when you're with a team. So, when you're practicing Kanban alone, it's best to apply what is relevant for you. A good suggestion for this is practicing the principles of implementing WIP limits and visualizing your workflow. But if you feel all core principles are relevant for you, you go right ahead and practice them. But understand first why you'll need them, and then proceed.

Conclusion

Kanban is an interesting system to be used for project management. From its humble beginnings as the system that would bring Toyota back into the game to its current form, it has brought a whole new way of managing projects for companies and offices.

Sure, it may have its ups and downs, its benefits and risks, and its oddities, but it cannot be denied that the results it brings can really make a difference. When you add the factor of scaling, ABC classification, other project management methods, and certification, it shows you that Kanban can be used in more ways than one.

It has also brought a whole new notion to what it really means to manage projects. After all, being able to visualize your workflow, set your limits, define policies, and manage tasks to achieve a fully completed project is truly a marvelous feat. To top it all off, Kanban can even be used on your own if you choose. It's a matter of taking the core principles and adapting them to any situation.

Further, there's the fact that Kanban has not only been used in physical form successfully but has also found success in digital form. It's been so successful in digital form that software development companies have made tools that streamline the Kanban method in a way that lets everyone have their own Kanban board with just a few clicks.

With that, this is your chance to take the first step to visualize what your workflow is and manage your projects the way they were meant to be. So, are you ready to get started and implement the Kanban method in your projects? Go for it! The stage is all yours.

Kanban is a challenging system to learn but when done right, it can help you out with your various projects. With that being said, you may find yourself eager to expand your horizons and learn what goes beyond the initial principles. Check out some of the things lined up for you below.

Where To Get Certified

While you are aware of the certifications that you can get with Kanban, you need to have an idea about where you can get them. The list below offers you various places for official certification.

- **LeanKanban University**

  If you're looking for a place to get the TKP and AKT certifications, LeanKanban University is where you'll need to go. LeanKanban is a website that provides a comprehensive system for getting the certification you aim to pursue.

  The TKP certification class they offer lasts for one day and you'll learn the essentials such as knowing how work is organized, improving your visibility, and more. You'll also learn more about the concepts of Kanban as well as learning how to be comfortable with a team.

  There are no prerequisites for this certification, so, as described in Chapter 9, all experience levels are welcome to apply for this one. Also, you'll receive the TKP credential once you're done.

As for the AKT certification class, it'll last for five days. Aside from being granted the ability to teach curriculum associated with Kanban, the AKT class is different from certification because this doesn't teach Kanban at all. Instead, it provides the opportunity for students like you to gather what you know about Kanban and present case studies to let the teachers know how well-versed you are in the method. In a way, it's the class that will make the student the trainer and you will be well-equipped to teach other students who desire to become a Kanban trainer.

A prerequisite for this class is that you're already certified as a KMP and have a case study about Kanban prepared.

When you've completed the class, you'll have the AKT credential and this will open up opportunities for offering your training services with organizations that need a trainer to teach Kanban.

- **IBQMI**

  Eager to be a Kanban Coaching Professional? IBQMI has the class for you. Though this option is going to be a bit costly, there are some great advantages that will give value for what you'll be spending on this, such as having a lifelong certificate, the official badge, and the authenticity that will indicate that you're a certified Kanban coach for life.

  The IBQMI Certified Kanban Coach™ certification provides many benefits. One of them is getting the best approach to understanding Kanban in the many industries it has been used for in the last several decades. It also provides the opportunity to apply what you'll be learning in other areas for better management.

The certification also gives the learner everything they need to know about the concepts of Kanban as well as knowing the difference between the Kanban methods, the significance of the Agile Kanban, knowing more about the principles that make up the Kanban system, how Kanban works in different scenarios, and more.

- **Agile42**

  Ready to get certified but want something more interactive and engaging? Agile42 has that and more. A section of the LeanKanban University, this offers its own approach to the KMP certification. For this one, you'll be attending a class that introduces you to Agile42's unique approach to teaching more about the Kanban method for two days.

  Known as the LeanKanban University KMP I Certification, you'll learn the ways of Kanban through games and activities that aim to give you a better understanding of how Kanban works without having to learn it the traditional way.

  It'll also let participants understand more about the ins and outs of Kanban as well as the intricacies and upsides and downsides to it.

  An advantage to this certification is participants will not only receive the certificate, but also a digital copy of the book titled *Kanban*, written by David J. Anderson, a listing in the university's directory, and proof of membership in LeanKanban University.

And after completing Agile42's LeanKanban University KMP I Certification, you'll have the opportunity to boost your level and pursue KMP II, if you so choose.

- **PROFESSIONAL SCRUM™ WITH KANBAN CERTIFICATION**

In Chapter 7, you learned a bit on how you can combine the method of Kanban with Scrum. If you're eager to really boost the combo, you can do so with this certification. Handled by Scrum.org, this certification gives you a chance to learn how Scrum works right from the start with Kanban applied to it. When you've become certified, you'll already have an idea on how teams using Scrum can make good use of Kanban in their existing workflow.

But before you go for this one, it must be understood that you'll need to take an assessment which is said to be intensive because you'll be asked a lot of questions that pertain to Kanban's use with the Scrum system. This means you can't just walk in and expect you're the expert: You need to have some knowledge on both systems and know how they can benefit.

Kanban Board Templates

When you're implementing Kanban, you'll be using the board a lot. As you have learned in Chapter 3, you can make your own. But if you're not in the mood to create one or you need some inspiration on how it can work for your various projects, below are some templates you can use.

- **Sales team board**

This Kanban board template is built for any projects involving sales. For this one, the three sections are named differently to indicate that this mainly for sales teams. The first section that usually says, "To Do" is labeled as "Qualifications." The second section that usually says "Doing" is labeled as "Proposal." Finally, the third section that usually says "Done" is labeled as "Sale."

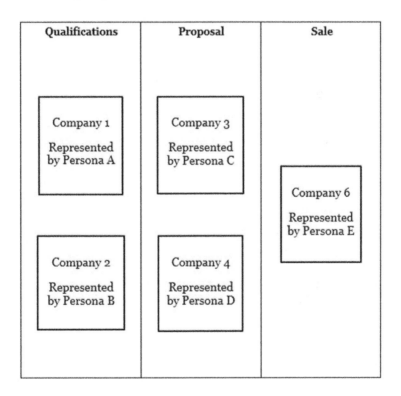

- **Design team board**

This template is built for projects that involve design. It doesn't differ much from the standard Kanban board, but the sections are titled differently. There's the "In Progress" section which is in place for "Doing" while "Complete" replaces "Done." This is a way for designers to be comfortable with the flow of things.

The template also gives another distinction from other templates: When you've completed a task, you can mark it by drawing a line over the text. This will give the signal that the tasks that were once in progress have been done and will now give way to more tasks.

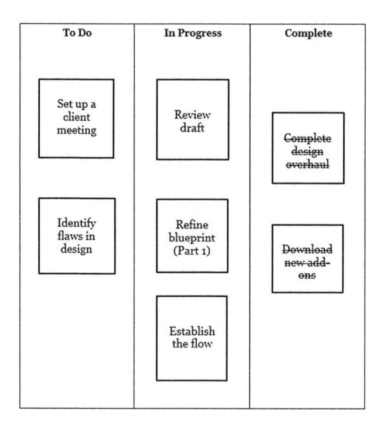

- **Software development board**

This board template resembles the design team board template from above, so there's not much of a difference. For this one, it is mainly designed for those managing projects involved in software development, so you can freely mark the tasks and processes unique to your project based on what your project is all about.

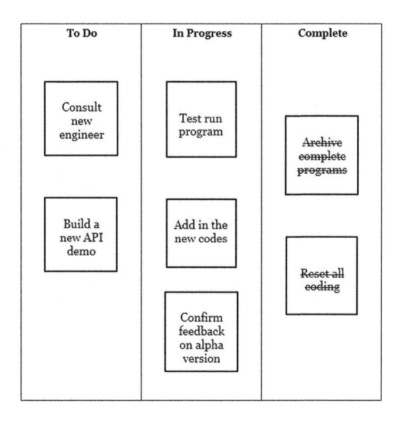

- **Business consultant board**

This board template, which is designed for projects involving business consulting, uses the same interface as the design team and software development board templates, so this won't be too much of a pain to use. As the example shows, you can mark many of the tasks accordingly.

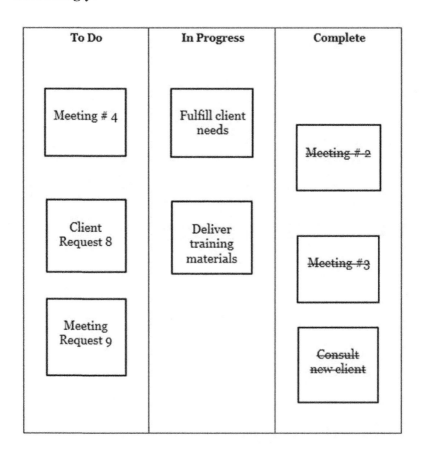

- **General tasks board**

  This template is versatile because it can be used with almost any project you can imagine. Using the basics of all board templates, you can simply put your task cards in the sections appropriately.

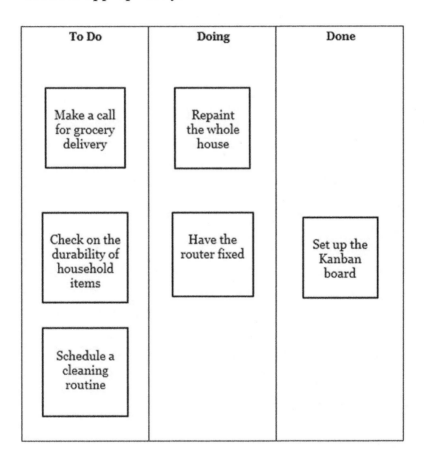

Where To Buy Materials For Your Physical Kanban Board

If you're the type who is more keen to use the physical Kanban board, you'll no doubt wonder where you can get materials for it. Sure, you might have some at home or at your office, but what if the supplies run out? You'll need a few places to go to when you need to restock. There are some places online where you can buy materials that make your board unique. Here are places to check when you're browsing online:

- **Etsy**

  This well-known craft website is very similar to eBay because it's the place where many craft-makers go to sell their materials at a great price. But much like eBay, you'll need to do a bit of homework and keep a close eye for any good prices that fit for your budget. But once you get used to it, you'll find the items you need to make sure your physical Kanban board is all good.

- **eBay**

  If you're eager to get your crafting materials through many listings and still get your bargain, then you can give eBay a try. A fair warning: You'll need to make sure you're only in it for crafting materials and not a bargain on some lucrative items that have nothing to do with making your Kanban board. So, try not to get distracted when going with this option.

- **Walmart**

  If you'd rather just buy your materials without having to go through so much bidding, you can try Walmart. This retailer has many of the materials you'll need when making your Kanban board. You can also check out some good deals from time to time.

- **Best Buy**

  Though this company is known for selling electronic products for businesses and consumers, it's also got some great office supplies on sale. This can be great for your physical Kanban board because you'll need some writing instruments and task cards to get yourself all set up with the board.

- **Create for Less**

  When you're in need of creating something that will give some good visual boosts to your physical Kanban board, head to Create for Less. This site has very great deals for the crafting materials you'll need. It also has exceptional customer service, so if you run into any issues, you can consult them for help.

Suggested Programs For Use With Kanban

Nowadays, you can use Kanban with the aid of technology. But what programs can you use? Here are the ones to take note of:

- **Microsoft Excel**

  When it comes to making a Kanban board from spreadsheets, look toward Microsoft Excel. This program, which is part of the Microsoft Office bundle, is a great tool to have when you're practicing Kanban because, with the many functions and formulas you can use, you'll be able to build a system that will help you fulfill your primary goals. The only downside with this is you'll be doing a lot of things manually since the formulas and other calculations you'll need to have must be made by you, but if you don't mind that, you'll be right at home with Microsoft Excel.

- **Evernote**

  It can seem like a weird choice to consider Evernote, a well-known note taking app for various devices, as a program for Kanban but with some creativity, it can be done. A good way this program can be used to apply what you've learned about Kanban is by using the note-taking features Evernote has to offer.

  Also, it can be beneficial to use this as your Kanban tool because Evernote syncs with all devices you log into. This means even when you need to leave your computer for a trip somewhere else, you can take a look at your digital Kanban board on your phone. It can be a bit of a drag when you have to edit your board after a task is done or when you have to add some items, but once you get used to it, you'll find Evernote will come in handy.

- **Kanban Tool**

  The name alone already tells you what it's all about. Kanban Tool is a software application that lets you create the ideal Kanban board for managing the tasks and workflow.

  This program has been suggested by many because its board view feature makes it easy for you to visualize and organize your projects. It also lets you arrange your tasks in various sections, add additional actions, and tweak the settings.

Another benefit with Kanban Tool is that it lets you set up your own server. This means that when you and your team need to get things done in a more controlled virtual environment, Kanban Tool has it covered for you.

The downside to this is that you'll need to pay a higher free to get some of the better features, but if you don't mind, you've got yourself a good deal.

- **ProjectManager.com**

Looking to use the program that deems itself the "ultimate Kanban board tool"? ProjectManager.com is the one for you. This program lives up to the title by providing everything you'll need when creating your Kanban board. It has many features you never thought you'd need such as time management features, real-time updating, and more. It's pretty much the Kanban board upgraded to the max. Why go for the ordinary when you can go for the extraordinary with this option?

The program's other features are definitely great, even for beginners. You'll be able to view a project's progress via the dashboard, assign tasks and set limits, type in comments, and attach files to the cards that have your tasks mapped out so that the context is better understood as you get the project done.

You can also integrate ProjectManager.com with other programs you may be using such as Google Apps and Microsoft Project. This will give you more freedom to share the board with your other team members when needed.

One of its best features is the reporting feature because it gives you the ability to gather different types of reports based on your preference. This means if you're not in the mood to be manual with your data, ProjectManager.com can do it for you automatically. But don't worry, you're free to customize the way you'll do your reporting if you still got it in you to manually gather data your way.

As for creating your workflow, it's got some great features to help you visualize how you'll like your project to go, ranging from toggling between the various task views and a comprehensive viewing feature.

In terms of price, ProjectManager.com's basic plan starts at $15 a month but you'll need to have at least four other users join you to get it up and running. But fret not, there's a 30-day trial, so you can see how this program will work for you and your team.

- **GitScrum**

  Judging by the name, it's easy to tell that this is a program designed for Scrum practitioners. But, conveniently enough, this one is designed for Kanban too. GitScrum is a new program that has many features that even the most established programs don't have such as the bug reports and the ability to track your logged in hours.

  GitScrum also provides tools to make Kanban more useful such as the boards and a calendar. You can even customize workflows based on your preferences for your projects. There's also the ability for you and the rest of the team to upload and share files and keep yourselves posted on how tasks are going through the progression of the project.

GitScrum can be integrated with other cool programs such as Dropbox, Trello, and Discord.

As for the price, this one has a free version for up to three users. Beyond that, you'll need to spend $12 a month for up to ten users.

- **Trello**

Trello is deemed one of the best tools for Kanban and for good reason: It's known for having many integrations with other programs that make it an indispensable aid to have. These programs include Google Drive, Evernote, and Slack.

Besides having the same features as other tools, Trello also has its own configuration settings so you can customize everything to your heart's content. But much like Kanban itself, this is not a ready-for-use method, so you'll have to have your plan in mind before you use this program because Trello doesn't have any preset templates for usage. So, if you're not the type to dig in and make the workflow the way you want it, you'd better steer clear of this one.

- **ZenHub**

ZenHub is another great program for Kanban. What makes it different from other programs is that it provides a surefire system that won't need much adjustment. This is especially true when you're using it with the well-known GitHub, which is designed to integrate with ZenHub in a lot of great ways. This is a timesaver because anything you've created in GitHub can be managed with ZenHub. It's also got the usual features you would expect such as automating workflows and migrating data when needed.

ZenHub's pricing is $5 a month per user. If you're not yet ready to pay, you can give its 14-day free trial a test run to see how it works for you.

- **Blossom**

  If your project is involved with software development and need a tool that is already designed to serve your needs right from the get-go, you can go with Blossom. This project management tool has been specially designed to help software development teams because its main features were all made with software development in mind. This means you don't have to make many customizations: The customizations have already been made for you.

  Just like ZenHub, Blossom can be integrated with GitHub so anything you've built in the latter can be managed easily. Also, if you'd like to have your team learn a bit more about Blossom, you can try the full training that Blossom offers.

  Sounds all good, right? You'll have to pay $19 a month for a team that consists of up to 5 members. However, there are free trials offered for all the plans, so you can see if Blossom is made for you.

- **Monday.com**

  They say Mondays are a drag. But Monday.com is anything but. This project management tool, which integrates many of Kanban's methods, principles, and features, does a lot of things to get you right into the heart of your project.

  Instead of putting in lots of features, it strips the unnecessary ones and goes with the essential tools that'll get you progress. You can think of it as the tool that strips away the fat and goes lean by boosting the essentials.

  Aside from this, Monday.com also has the ability to let you manage multiple boards, being able to attach files to marked cards and gather data from boards to archive a data collection that can be used for future projects.

- **Breeze**

  If you're the type who just likes having a program that has the essential features with a simple interface, Breeze is the one for you. This project management program doesn't get cluttered with features and instead goes for the ones that are essential, similar to Blossom. But it goes beyond that and makes sure that the tools you'll need are the critical ones. You won't find the fancy features seen in other programs, so don't expect it to trump everything.

  The downside to Breeze is it's a bit pricey, starting at $29 a month per user, but it does have a free trial version to try.

- **JIRA**

  Want the program that has been proven successful with many IT companies all around the world? Go with JIRA. This Kanban board tool has all the features you'll need to assemble your board and add greatness to it. It even lets you keep track of any issues that might come along the project and grants you various views that will surely benefit you in the long run.

  Just like the other programs listed above, JIRA can be integrated with over 3,000 apps and can be customized to your preference.

  The pricing for this software is reasonable too, with the standard package having you pay just $7 a month for up to 100 users and a 7-day trial if you want to see how it works.

Best Kanban Blogs

Kanban is an ever-growing management method, so it goes without saying that many people are using it to get to the results they want. That's why if you're eager to learn what's going on in the Kanban scene, there are blogs that are up to date on the news. Here are some of them:

- **Discovery Kanban**

  This blog, which was set up by Patrick Steyaert, is written from the perspective of a Lean Agile coach who provides his opinion on Kanban and the developments going on in different industries. When you're in doubt about Kanban's development, or you just need some fresh perspective, this blog has you covered.

- **Hakan Forss's Blog**

  Created by Hakan Forss (hence the blog's title), this blog may look a little bit ordinary, but a closer look shows Hakan is, just like Patrick Steyaert, an Agile coach who helps develop the best ways to get projects done and provides great views on how effective Kanban can be.

- **AvailAgility**

  This blog was set up by Karl Scotland, a software practitioner who currently holds a position as a Lean Agile consultant and has 15 years of experience. He writes about his experiences as well as interesting and great posts about Kanban.

- **David J Anderson & Associations, Inc.**

  This blog is considered one of the best to read because its founder is David J. Anderson. His name may not be familiar to you, but for others he's famous because he was the man who took the idea of Kanban and adapted it in a way that had everybody raving about it for a long time. If you need a little refresher on how today's Kanban methods work, this blog is for you.

- **Becoming an Agile Family**

  Blog creator Maritza van den Heuvel makes interesting posts about Kanban has improved her life as a mother and is able to give a fresh take on how Kanban and Agile can work for you. Though it's no longer getting updates since Maritza said farewell, you can still give it a read from time to time.

Additional Reading For Kanban

While you are reading this eBook to get yourself started with the Kanban method, you may find yourself wanting to advance your knowledge. Maybe the certifications are a bit too much for your budget, so you'd like a little peek into what the higher levels offer. Don't worry, there are other books you can try that will expand your Kanban knowledge further.

- **Kanban From The Inside (Mike Burrows)**

  Written for leaders who look to deepen what they know of Kanban, this book will give you a new way to see Kanban because the author ups the game and provides new concepts that will have you see that Kanban is more than just what you learned in this eBook.

- **Personal Kanban: Mapping Work – Navigating Life (Jim Benson)**

  Chapter 10 showed you that Kanban can be done solo, so if you're interested to further that practice, you can give this book a try. It takes two core principles of the Kanban method and shows you how to apply them to your own personal life. It may seem impossible at first but after reading the success stories, who says there can't be a way to make Kanban work for your life?

- **Kanban Change Leadership (Klaus Leopold)**

  This book, which David J. Anderson has recommended, shows you how Kanban can be used for leadership. It also provides many insights on how change can be implemented effectively in the workplace and more.

- **Real World Kanban: Do Less, Accomplish More with Lean Thinking (Mattias Skarin)**

  In Chapter 5, you learned about how Kanban has been applied in the real world to let you know it's not just a bunch of words and theories all mushed up together. That's why with this book you'll read up on four case studies that show you more of the success Kanban can provide. You'll also see images of the Kanban boards that were used and see how Kanban can bring together organizations to complete the projects they set out to do.

- **Stop Starting, Start Finishing (Arne Roock)**

  Need a book that can get you started with the principle of setting WIPs while having a little fun? Get this book, which is actually a cute little comic booklet that was written to introduce the ways of Kanban and Lean. It also includes a great take on the core principles so that you'll know what to do when applying Kanban to various projects.

- **Kanban (David J. Anderson)**

  If you always wondered how Kanban became the trend with software developments in the last decade, you can check this book out. Written by David J. Anderson, the author took the concept of Kanban and somehow modernized it. It can be crazy to think that the Kanban approach would be much use in software development, but after many years it shows even IT departments have some use for the method.

References

31 Practical Kanban Board Examples. (n.d.). Retrieved from https://kanbanize.com/kanban-resources/kanban-software/kanban-board-examples/

AKT Class. (n.d.). Retrieved from https://leankanban.com/akt-program/

Aston, B. (2019). Improve Your Workflow: 10 Best Kanban Tools of 2019 (Trello Alternative). Retrieved from https://thedigitalprojectmanager.com/best-trello-alternatives-top-kanban-tools/

Ballé, M. (2018). Is kanban relevant to office work? Retrieved from https://www.lean.org/balle/DisplayObject.cfm?o=3612

Benson, J. (2017). Six Personal Kanban Habits to Avoid. Retrieved from https://www.lean.org/LeanPost/Posting.cfm?LeanPostId=675

Boiser, L. (2019). Avoid Common Project Management Mistakes by Using Kanban. Retrieved from https://kanbanzone.com/2019/project-management-mistakes-avoided-with-kanban/

Boiser, L. (2019). Kanban for Improved Office Productivity. Retrieved from https://kanbanzone.com/2019/kanban-improved-office-productivity/

Bose, J. (2018). What Are The Most Valuable Kanban Certifications? Retrieved from https://www.knowledgehut.com/blog/agile/what-are-the-most-valuable-kanban-certifications

Craftybird. (2018). 10 Great Websites to Buy Cheap Craft Materials Online. Retrieved from https://feltmagnet.com/crafts/Great-Websites-to-Buy-Cheap-Craft-Materials

Cote, A. (2018). 12 Kanban Board Examples for Beginners. Retrieved from https://www.paymoapp.com/blog/kanban-board-examples-for-freelancers-and-teams/

Digite Inc. (2017). Implementing a Successful Kanban System for Manufacturing and Inventory Management. Retrieved from https://medium.com/@digite/implementing-a-successful-kanban-system-for-manufacturing-and-inventory-management-be6d27147986

Ease Your Project Stress With These Kanban Lessons. (n.d.). Retrieved from http://www.smartprojex.com/ease-your-project-stress-with-these-kanban-lessons/

Griffin, K. (2016). Top 5 Kanban Books to Add to Your Reading List. Retrieved from https://leankit.com/blog/2016/09/top-5-kanban-books-add-reading-list/

Guay, M. (2017). The 11 Best Kanban Apps to Build Your Own Productivity Workflow. Retrieved from https://zapier.com/blog/best-kanban-apps/

History of Kanban. (n.d.). Retrieved from
https://agilerasmus.com/wordpress/history-of-kanban/

How To Scale Kanban Well? (2015). Retrieved from
https://kanbantool.com/blog/how-to-scale-kanban-well

Huffman, S. (2018). Do's and Don'ts: Use a Kanban Board!
(Part 1). Retrieved from
https://www.mpug.com/articles/dos-donts-use-kanban-
board-part-1/

Jacobson, G. (2018). The Pros AND Cons of Digital Kanban
Boards. Retrieved from
https://blog.kainexus.com/improvement-
disciplines/lean/kanban/kanban-boards/the-pros-and-cons-
of-digital-kanban-boards

Jeremy. (2016). 3 tips to set up an efficient Kanban board.
Retrieved from
https://kantree.io/blog/tips/2016/08/kanban-board

Kanban Board. (n.d.). Retrieved from
https://www.smartdraw.com/kanban-board/

Kanban Explained For Beginners. (n.d.). Retrieved from
https://kanbanize.com/kanban-resources/getting-
started/what-is-kanban/

Kanban Library: David J Anderson's Picks. (n.d.). Retrieved
from https://kanbanize.com/kanban-resources/kanban-
library/david-j-andersons-picks/

Kanban Management Professional (KMP) Training. (2019). Retrieved from https://www.agile42.com/en/training/kmp-kanban-management-professional-training/

Kanban Misconceptions and Myths. (2018). Retrieved from https://kanbantool.com/blog/kanban-misconceptions-and-myths

Kanban Project Management. (2016). Retrieved from https://www.kanbanchi.com/kanban-project-management

Kanban dos and don'ts. (2014). Retrieved from https://thinkpurpose.com/2014/03/10/kanban-dos-and-donts/

Kanban system. (n.d.). Retrieved from https://workerbase.com/kanban-system/

Kanban vs. Scrum: What are the differences? (n.d.). Retrieved from https://leankit.com/learn/kanban/kanban-vs-scrum/

Kanban. (n.d.). Retrieved from https://leanmanufacturingtools.org/kanban/

Kurzawska, K. (2018). Which Software With Kanban Board Is Worth Using? Retrieved from https://www.timecamp.com/blog/2018/08/kanban-board-software/

Lasovski, J. (2011). English: A Scrum board suggesting to use Kanban. Retrieved from https://en.wikipedia.org/wiki/File:Simple-kanban-board-.jpg

Lawless, S. (2019). How To Create An Efficient Kanban Board/Process. Retrieved from https://purplegriffon.com/blog/create-kanban-board-process

Leanability. (2014). Scaling Kanban. Retrieved from https://www.leanability.com/en/blog-en/2014/09/scaling-kanban-2/

Leankor. (n.d.). Right and Wrong Way To Set Up Your Kanban Boards. Retrieved from https://www.leankor.com/right-and-wrong-setup-kanban-boards/

Lyles, A. (2018). 8 Step ABC Inventory Analysis and Classification Process. Retrieved from https://falconfastening.com/lean-learning/vmi-vendor-managed-inventory/8-step-abc-inventory-analysis-classification-process-1-of-3-abc-class-definitions/

Mancera, L. (2016). The 10 Best Sites For Office Supplies. Retrieved from https://www.classycareergirl.com/2016/05/office-supplies/

Majowska, A. (2015). What Problems Do You Have With Kanban? Retrieved from https://dzone.com/articles/problems-with-kanban

Maximize Your Time, Improve Efficiency with the Kanban System. (n.d.). Retrieved from https://leankit.com/learn/kanban/kanban-system/

Naydenov, P. (2018). 6 Reasons You May Fail with Kanban Implementation. Retrieved from https://kanbanize.com/blog/problems-with-kanban-implementation/

Nevogt, D. (2019). Kanban Project Management: Everything You Need to Know. Retrieved from https://blog.hubstaff.com/kanban-project-management/

Parker, S. (2018). The 14 Best Kanban Apps | Free Kanban Software & Tools of 2019. Retrieved from https://productivityland.com/best-kanban-apps/

PROFESSIONAL SCRUM™ WITH KANBAN CERTIFICATION. (n.d.). Retrieved from https://www.scrum.org/professional-scrum-with-kanban-certification

Powell-Morse, A. (2017). Extreme Programming: What Is It And How Do You Use It? Retrieved from https://airbrake.io/blog/sdlc/extreme-programming

Radigan, D. (n.d.). Kanban - A brief introduction. Retrieved from https://www.atlassian.com/agile/kanban

Rebbel, C. (2019). How To Computer Kanban Sizes. Retrieved from https://bizfluent.com/how-6509376-compute-kanban-sizes.html

Rehkopf, M. (n.d.). Kanban vs Scrum. Retrieved from https://www.atlassian.com/agile/kanban/kanban-vs-scrum

Sands, B. (n.d.). How To Earn Kanban Certification. Retrieved from https://study.com/academy/popular/how-to-earn-kanban-certification.html

Sergeev, A. (2016). Types of Kanban System. Retrieved from https://hygger.io/blog/two-types-of-kanban-systems/

Sergeev, A. (2019). What Makes Kanban Popular in 2019? Basic Facts You've Wanted To Know. https://medium.com/swlh/what-makes-kanban-popular-in-2019-basic-facts-youve-wanted-to-know-de5b31a02373

Shmula Contributor. (2017). Digital vs Physical Kanban Boards. Retrieved from https://www.shmula.com/digital-vs-physical-kanban-boards/22755/

Shmula Contributor. (2017). Simple Kanban Systems to Setup at Home. Retrieved from https://www.shmula.com/simple-kanban-systems-to-setup-at-home/22575/

Shoo, D. (2017). Kanban Disadvantages. Retrieved from https://bizfluent.com/list-7543857-kanban-disadvantages.html

Siderova, S. (2018). The Top 10 Benefits of Kanban. Retrieved from https://getnave.com/blog/kanban-benefits/

Six Types of Kanban Explained. (n.d.). Retrieved from https://news.ibqmi.org/six-types-of-kanban-explained

Stuart, J. & Perez, M. (n.d.). 5 Misconceptions About Kanban. Retrieved from https://www.construx.com/resources/5-misconceptions-about-kanban/

Team Kanban Practitioner. (n.d.). Retrieved from https://leankanban.com/team-kanban/

Terry, J. (n.d.). What Is Kanban? Retrieved from https://www.planview.com/resources/articles/what-is-kanban/

The original Certified Kanban Coach. (n.d.). Retrieved from https://www.ibqmi.org/certifications/certified-kanban-coach

Timmins, J. (n.d.). Kanban vs MRP: The Answer Rests in Your Forecasting Skills. Retrieved from https://www.teamacuity.biz/blog/kanban-vs-mrp-the-answer-rests-in-your-forecasting-skills

Top Kanban Blogs. (n.d.). Retrieved from https://leankit.com/learn/kanban/top-kanban-blogs/

Understanding Kanban Inventory Management and Its Uses Across Multiple Industries. (n.d.). Retrieved from https://www.smartsheet.com/understanding-kanban-inventory-management-and-its-uses-across-multiple-industries

What Is Kanban? (n.d.). Retrieved from https://kanbanzone.com/kanban-resources/what-is-kanban/

What Is Kanban? (n.d.). Retrieved from
https://www.digite.com/kanban/what-is-kanban/

What Is Kanban? An Introduction to Kanban Methodology.
(n.d.). Retrieved from https://resources.collab.net/agile-
101/what-is-kanban

What Is Kanban? Comprehensive Overview of the Kanban
Method. (n.d.). Retrieved from
https://www.digite.com/kanban/what-is-kanban/

What Is The Difference Between Scrum, Kanban And XP?
(n.d.). Retrieved from
http://www.softwaretestingclass.com/what-is-the-
difference-between-scrum-kanban-and-xp/

Wikipedia contributors. (2019). Kanban. Retrieved from
https://en.wikipedia.org/w/index.php?title=Kanban&oldid=
917015543

Wingfield, T. (2010). Doing Kanban Wrong. Retrieved from
https://www.infoq.com/articles/doing-kanban-wrong/

Printed in Great Britain
by Amazon